Daily

GRADE 4

Language

Review

Editorial Development: Carrie Gwynne
Lisa Vitarisi Mathews
Copy Editing: Laurie Westrich
Art Direction: Cheryl Puckett
Design/Production: Carolina Caird

EMC 582

Visit
teaching-standards.com
to view a correlation
of this book.
This is a free service.

**Correlated to
Current Standards**

For information about other Evan-Moor products, call 1-800-777-4362,
fax 1-800-777-4332, or visit our website, www.evan-moor.com.
Entire contents © 2015 EVAN-MOOR CORP.
18 Lower Ragsdale Drive, Monterey, CA 93940-5746. Printed in USA.

CPSIA: McNaughton & Gunn, Saline, MI USA [7/2020]

What's in the new *Daily Language Review*

This revised edition of *Daily Language Review* has been updated to cover and support the current standards and methodologies. This edition focuses on the following:

- expanding useful academic and idiomatic vocabulary
- *using* language, not just identifying elements of language
- practicing language in the context of reading and writing, not in isolation

To reflect current methodologies, *Daily Language Review* now provides

Increased vocabulary practice:

- word choice
- word relationships
- multiple vocabulary strategies
- writing sentences with new vocabulary

Items using context sentences:

- editing sentences
- completing sentences
- writing sentences

Daily topic focus:

- represents more authentic classroom-related uses of language

Exposure to sentences from a variety of writing types:

- informational
- narrative

What's in
Daily Language Review

Days 1 through 4
Conventions of Standard English

Half-page activities offer scaffolded practice of grade-specific, standards-based skills. Each day's activity includes four language items:

- two sentence-editing exercises
- two items that practice a variety of language and vocabulary skills

Day 5
Vocabulary Acquisition and Use

A full-page activity provides more extensive practice of a specific vocabulary strategy or skill and provides students the opportunity to practice using the words in their own sentences.

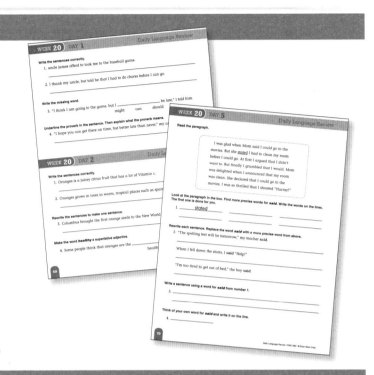

Additional Features

Skills Scope and Sequence

The chart on pages 6 and 7 lists the skills practiced in the daily activities for each week.

My Progress Chart and
My New Vocabulary Log

Students can monitor their own progress by recording and analyzing their daily scores and keeping track of new vocabulary words they are learning. Reproduce and distribute to students the My Progress chart and the My New Vocabulary log.

Answer Key

The answer key provides sample responses for each day's activity. For many of the open-ended items, other answers are possible. Accept any response that produces correct language and follows the directions. The answer key begins on page 119.

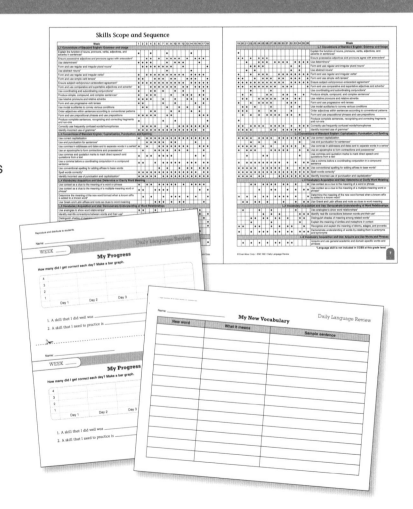

How to Use
Daily Language Review

1. Reproduce the activities for each five-day unit and cut apart the half-page lessons for Days 1 through 4, or distribute a student book to each student. If appropriate, provide access to a dictionary and a thesaurus.

2. Consult the Skills Scope and Sequence chart (pages 6 and 7) to identify any skills that are unfamiliar to your students. You may want to preview those skills as a whole-class activity.

3. Have students work to complete the daily lessons individually, with a partner, or in a small group. You may want to use each day's lesson as a quick informal assessment.

4. Establish a procedure for students to complete and check their own work. For example, read over the steps in the how-to tips below.

5. Allow sufficient time for sharing responses and discussing word choices. Elicit a range of answers for the open-ended items. Modeling a variety of strategies and thought processes offers valuable learning benefits.

 Reproduce and distribute to students.

How to Correct the Sentences

1. Read each sentence. Think about what it says.

2. Look for mistakes in spelling, punctuation, grammar, and word choice.

3. **Hint:** You may need to add, change, or take out a word or add punctuation.

4. Rewrite each sentence neatly on the line, on the back of the sheet, or on a separate sheet of paper.

5. Reread your new sentence. Does it make sense and sound right?

How to Answer the Vocabulary Questions

1. Read each sentence. Think about what it says.

2. To choose a word, think about what each choice means and how it is usually used. If needed, change the word to make it agree with the subject or the tense.

3. To understand a word with a prefix or suffix, divide the word and think about each part separately. Then figure out how the prefix or suffix changes the root word.

4. To figure out the meaning of an unknown word, look for context clues in the sentence.

5. Reread the sentence. Does the word or meaning make sense in the sentence?

Skills Scope and Sequence

Week	1	2	3	4	5	6	7	8	9	10	11	12	13	14	15	16	17	18
L.1 Conventions of Standard English: Grammar and Usage																		
Explain the function of nouns, pronouns, verbs, adjectives, and adverbs in sentences	●			●				●					●					
Ensure possessive adjectives and pronouns agree with antecedent			●	●		●		●	●	●	●		●		●	●	●	
Use determiners	●	●	●	●				●		●	●	●			●			
Form and use regular and irregular plural nouns			●	●	●	●	●	●	●	●		●						●
Use abstract nouns								●						●				
Form and use regular and irregular verbs	●		●	●	●	●	●	●	●	●	●	●		●	●	●	●	
Form and use simple verb tenses	●	●			●	●		●	●		●	●	●	●				●
Ensure subject-verb/pronoun-antecedent agreement	●	●	●		●	●	●	●	●	●	●	●		●	●	●	●	●
Form and use comparative and superlative adjectives and adverbs	●		●	●	●	●	●	●			●	●		●	●		●	●
Use coordinating and subordinating conjunctions	●		●	●		●	●			●		●					●	
Produce simple, compound, and complex sentences	●		●	●	●				●			●	●	●		●	●	
Use relative pronouns and relative adverbs	●	●	●	●			●			●			●	●			●	●
Form and use progressive verb tenses	●	●					●			●				●			●	
Use modal auxiliaries to convey various conditions			●	●				●			●		●		●			
Order adjectives within sentences according to conventional patterns				●	●				●			●			●	●		
Form and use prepositional phrases and use prepositions	●	●	●	●				●	●							●	●	●
Produce complete sentences, recognizing and correcting fragments and run-ons	●						●			●								●
Correctly use frequently confused words/homophones			●	●	●	●					●		●		●			
Identify incorrect use of grammar	●	●	●	●	●	●	●	●	●	●	●	●	●	●		●		
L.2 Conventions of Standard English: Capitalization, Punctuation, and Spelling																		
Use correct capitalization	●		●	●	●	●	●	●	●	●	●	●	●	●	●	●	●	●
Use end punctuation for sentences			●	●	●	●	●		●	●				●				
Use commas in addresses and dates and to separate words in a series	●		●			●	●	●	●	●	●	●				●	●	●
Use an apostrophe to form contractions and possessives		●			●	●	●	●		●	●	●				●		
Use commas and quotation marks to mark direct speech and quotations from a text	●		●	●		●	●	●	●				●		●			
Use a comma before a coordinating conjunction in a compound sentence	●	●			●		●		●				●	●	●		●	●
Use conventional spelling for adding affixes to base words						●		●			●		●	●		●	●	●
Spell words correctly	●		●	●	●	●	●	●	●	●	●	●	●	●	●	●	●	●
Identify incorrect use of punctuation and capitalization	●	●	●	●		●		●	●	●	●	●	●	●		●		
L.4 Vocabulary Acquisition and Use: Determine or Clarify Word Meaning																		
Use context as a clue to the meaning of a word or phrase	●		●	●		●	●	●	●		●		●	●	●	●		
Use context as a clue to the meaning of a multiple-meaning word or phrase	●	●		●	●	●	●	●								●		●
Determine the meaning of the new word formed when a known affix is added to a known word		●		●			●		●	●	●		●		●			●
Use Greek and Latin affixes and roots as clues to word meaning					●	●	●		●		●	●					●	
L.5 Vocabulary Acquisition and Use: Demonstrate Understanding of Word Relationships																		
Use analogies to show word relationships	●	●			●						●			●				
Identify real-life connections between words and their use		●							●		●	●		●	●	●		●
Distinguish shades of meaning among related words			●			●		●	●		●	●	●		●	●		
Explain the meaning of similes and metaphors in context											●		●	●				●
Recognize and explain the meaning of idioms, adages, and proverbs						●			●	●	●							●
Demonstrate understanding of words by relating them to antonyms and synonyms		●									●	●	●	●	●	●	●	
L.6 Vocabulary Acquisition and Use: Acquire and Use Words and Phrases																		
Acquire and use general academic and domain-specific words and phrases													●		●			●

19	20	21	22	23	24	25	26	27	28	29	30	31	32	33	34	35	36	Week
																		L.1 Conventions of Standard English: Grammar and Usage
●																		Explain the function of nouns, pronouns, verbs, adjectives, and adverbs in sentences
●	●		●		●	●	●											Ensure possessive adjectives and pronouns agree with antecedent
		●			●	●	●		●	●	●	●		●	●	●	●	Use determiners
			●	●	●	●							●		●			Form and use regular and irregular plural nouns
		●		●									●		●			Use abstract nouns
●			●		●	●	●			●	●	●	●	●	●	●	●	Form and use regular and irregular verbs
●	●		●		●	●	●	●		●	●		●	●	●		●	Form and use simple verb tenses
●	●	●	●	●	●	●	●	●	●	●	●		●	●	●	●	●	Ensure subject-verb/pronoun-antecedent agreement
●	●		●	●		●	●	●	●		●	●	●				●	Form and use comparative and superlative adjectives and adverbs
			●					●										Use coordinating and subordinating conjunctions
	●		●			●	●			●	●		●		●			Produce simple, compound, and complex sentences
	●	●			●	●	●	●	●		●	●		●	●			Use relative pronouns and relative adverbs
●			●		●	●	●	●					●	●	●			Form and use progressive verb tenses
	●	●		●				●					●		●			Use modal auxiliaries to convey various conditions
●	●	●			●			●	●				●					Order adjectives within sentences according to conventional patterns
	●		●		●		●	●	●	●			●	●		●		Form and use prepositional phrases and use prepositions
●																		Produce complete sentences, recognizing and correcting fragments and run-ons
●	●		●	●	●	●		●	●	●	●		●		●	●	●	Correctly use frequently confused words/homophones
●	●	●	●					●	●		●	●	●	●	●			Identify incorrect use of grammar
																		L.2 Conventions of Standard English: Capitalization, Punctuation, and Spelling
●	●	●	●		●	●	●	●		●	●	●	●	●	●	●	●	Use correct capitalization
		●		●			●							●				Use end punctuation for sentences
●	●	●	●	●		●		●			●	●	●	●		●		Use commas in addresses and dates and to separate words in a series
●		●	●	●				●	●	●	●	●			●		●	Use an apostrophe to form contractions and possessives
	●			●	●									●				Use commas and quotation marks to mark direct speech and quotations from a text
●		●	●	●	●	●	●	●		●		●		●		●	●	Use a comma before a coordinating conjunction in a compound sentence
●	●	●	●	●		●	●		●	●	●		●		●	●	●	Use conventional spelling for adding affixes to base words
●	●	●	●	●	●	●	●	●	●	●	●	●	●	●	●	●	●	Spell words correctly
●	●	●	●		●	●				●	●	●	●	●	●	●	●	Identify incorrect use of punctuation and capitalization
																		L.4 Vocabulary Acquisition and Use: Determine or Clarify Word Meaning
		●	●		●	●	●	●		●	●		●				●	Use context as a clue to the meaning of a word or phrase
				●			●	●			●		●			●	●	Use context as a clue to the meaning of a multiple-meaning word or phrase
●		●		●		●	●		●	●	●	●		●			●	Determine the meaning of the new word formed when a known affix is added to a known word
	●	●		●	●		●				●			●		●	●	Use Greek and Latin affixes and roots as clues to word meaning
																		L.5 Vocabulary Acquisition and Use: Demonstrate Understanding of Word Relationships
	●				●			●					●					Use analogies to show word relationships
						●		●		●					●	●	●	Identify real-life connections between words and their use
			●	●		●	●			●	●		●		●	●		Distinguish shades of meaning among related words
			●					●						●				Explain the meaning of similes and metaphors in context
●	●			●	●			●		●			●	●		●		Recognize and explain the meaning of idioms, adages, and proverbs
●			●		●	●				●	●		●	●		●	●	Demonstrate understanding of words by relating them to antonyms and synonyms
																		L.6 Vocabulary Acquisition and Use: Acquire and Use Words and Phrases
	●		●		●		●			●	●		●	●				Acquire and use general academic and domain-specific words and phrases

Downloadable Detailed Skills List

For each of the 36 weeks of daily practice, there is an item-by-item list of the skills practiced along with sample responses. This is a free downloadable resource. See the inside front cover of this book for instructions on how to download.

The whole week on one page

Sample responses

Itemized skills are listed to help you monitor students' competencies

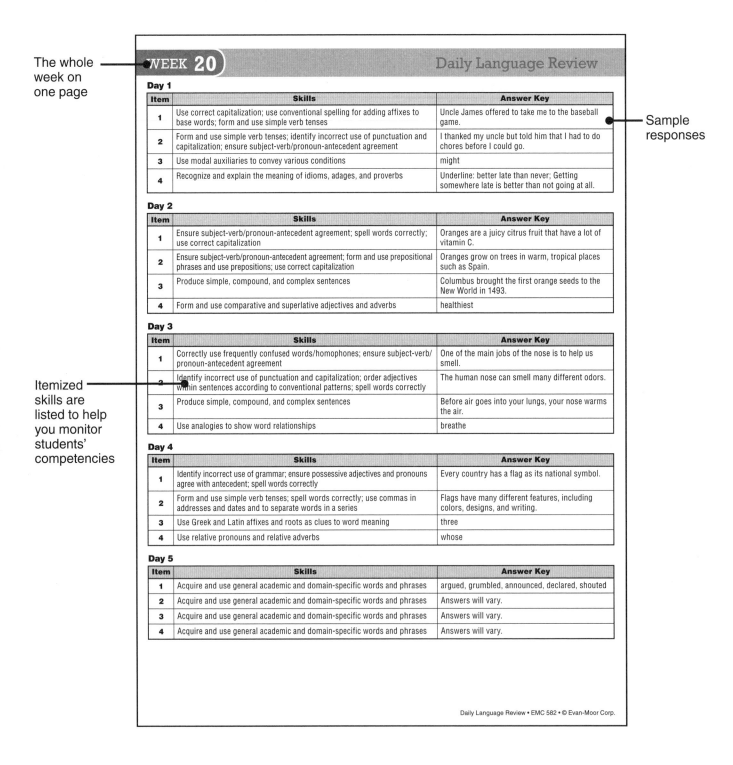

WEEK 20 — Daily Language Review

Day 1

Item	Skills	Answer Key
1	Use correct capitalization; use conventional spelling for adding affixes to base words; form and use simple verb tenses	Uncle James offered to take me to the baseball game.
2	Form and use simple verb tenses; identify incorrect use of punctuation and capitalization; ensure subject-verb/pronoun-antecedent agreement	I thanked my uncle but told him that I had to do chores before I could go.
3	Use modal auxiliaries to convey various conditions	might
4	Recognize and explain the meaning of idioms, adages, and proverbs	Underline: better late than never; Getting somewhere late is better than not going at all.

Day 2

Item	Skills	Answer Key
1	Ensure subject-verb/pronoun-antecedent agreement; spell words correctly; use correct capitalization	Oranges are a juicy citrus fruit that have a lot of vitamin C.
2	Ensure subject-verb/pronoun-antecedent agreement; form and use prepositional phrases and use prepositions; use correct capitalization	Oranges grow on trees in warm, tropical places such as Spain.
3	Produce simple, compound, and complex sentences	Columbus brought the first orange seeds to the New World in 1493.
4	Form and use comparative and superlative adjectives and adverbs	healthiest

Day 3

Item	Skills	Answer Key
1	Correctly use frequently confused words/homophones; ensure subject-verb/pronoun-antecedent agreement	One of the main jobs of the nose is to help us smell.
2	Identify incorrect use of punctuation and capitalization; order adjectives within sentences according to conventional patterns; spell words correctly	The human nose can smell many different odors.
3	Produce simple, compound, and complex sentences	Before air goes into your lungs, your nose warms the air.
4	Use analogies to show word relationships	breathe

Day 4

Item	Skills	Answer Key
1	Identify incorrect use of grammar; ensure possessive adjectives and pronouns agree with antecedent; spell words correctly	Every country has a flag as its national symbol.
2	Form and use simple verb tenses; spell words correctly; use commas in addresses and dates and to separate words in a series	Flags have many different features, including colors, designs, and writing.
3	Use Greek and Latin affixes and roots as clues to word meaning	three
4	Use relative pronouns and relative adverbs	whose

Day 5

Item	Skills	Answer Key
1	Acquire and use general academic and domain-specific words and phrases	argued, grumbled, announced, declared, shouted
2	Acquire and use general academic and domain-specific words and phrases	Answers will vary.
3	Acquire and use general academic and domain-specific words and phrases	Answers will vary.
4	Acquire and use general academic and domain-specific words and phrases	Answers will vary.

Daily Language Review • EMC 582 • © Evan-Moor Corp.

Name: _____

WEEK _____   Daily Language Review

My Progress

How many did I get correct each day? Make a bar graph.

4					
3					
2					
1					
	Day 1	Day 2	Day 3	Day 4	Day 5

1. A skill that I did well was _____.

2. A skill that I need to practice is _____.

✂ -

Name: _____

WEEK _____   Daily Language Review

My Progress

How many did I get correct each day? Make a bar graph.

4					
3					
2					
1					
	Day 1	Day 2	Day 3	Day 4	Day 5

1. A skill that I did well was _____.

2. A skill that I need to practice is _____.

Name: _____

My New Vocabulary

New word	What it means	Sample sentence

Write the sentences correctly.

1. "I seen an giant balloon in the sky this morning," Ben said.

2. "It were shinny and shape like an egg," he say.

Rewrite the sentence so it is not a run-on sentence.

3. "That was a blimp you saw it was part of a parade," I told Ben.

Add punctuation to the sentence.

4. The blimp is named *Spirit of America* I said.

Write the sentences correctly.

1. A curcus is a group of much performers animals and clowns.

2. If you go at a circus you mite see clowns who is act silly.

Rewrite the sentences to make a compound sentence. Use a comma and the word *and*.

3. You will see colorful costumes at a circus. You will also hear loud music there.

Use context clues to figure out the meaning of the bold word. Then write the meaning on the line.

4. Circus **vendors** sell popcorn, peanuts, and drinks to the crowd.

Write the sentences correctly.

1. Americans eat much Ice Cream then anyone else in the world.

   _____

2. Vanilla, Chocolate, and Strawberry are popular flavers but the popularest is vanilla.

   _____

Identify the part of speech of the bold words. Explain what the words do in the sentence.

3. Ice cream is a **cold**, **sweet**, and **creamy** treat that tastes good on a hot summer day.

   Part of speech: _____

   Explain: _____

Complete the analogy.

4. ice cream : creamy :: popcorn : _____

Write the sentences correctly.

1. My mom don't eat no meet and that makes she a vegetarian.

   _____

2. Some times mom eat rice and beens or spagetti with tomatoe sauce.

   _____

Rewrite the sentences to make a compound sentence. Use a comma and the word *but*.

3. Mom eats lots of veggies. She doesn't get bored because they are so tasty.

   _____

Write the missing word.

4. The vegetable _____ Mom and I like best is broccoli.

   　　　　who　　　　that　　　　which

Read the bold word and its different meanings.

> **roll**   a. bread that has been baked into a small piece
>
> b. to move on wheels or rollers
>
> c. to move one's body by turning over and over

Which meaning of *roll* is used in the sentence? Write the letter on the line.

1. In school we learned to stop, drop, and roll if there is a fire.   _____

2. My skateboard rolled down the hill.   _____

3. Every morning, Dad likes to have a cinnamon roll with his coffee.   _____

Write a paragraph using two of the meanings of the word *roll*.

4. _____

_____

_____

_____

_____

_____

Write the sentences correctly.

1. Many childs ride onto a bus every day.

   _____

2. Its important to stay in youse seat when an bus is moving.

   _____

Write the missing word.

3. There is a law that buses _____ stop at railroad tracks.

   must   should   can

4. People who drive buses must be very _____ drivers.

   helpful   friendly   careful

Write the sentences correctly.

1. My Grandma made me a party dress and she made me the school dress.

   _____

2. The dress for mine party have big purple polka dots.

   _____

Draw a line between the prefix and the root word of the underlined word. Then write the meaning on the line.

3. My sister spilled paint on my school dress, so I am <u>unable</u> to wear it.

   _____

Circle the meaning of the bold word.

4. I know my sister didn't **mean** to ruin my dress.

   a. unkind, selfish   b. to do on purpose

Write the sentences correctly.

1. Ride a bike is fun but there is many rools you have to follow.

_____

2. You must always where a helmut, whether you ride slowly or quick.

_____

Draw a line between the prefix and the root word of the underlined word. Then write the meaning on the line.

3. Before you ride your bike next time, you should <u>review</u> the rules.

_____

Complete the analogy.

4. rules : follow :: helmet : _____

Write the sentences correctly.

1. You should wore the right kind of shoes when you plays Soccer.

_____

2. If your shoes dont fit good, you mite get hurt in the soccer field.

_____

Write the missing word.

3. You _____ get blisters if you wear the wrong size shoes.

    could   must   should

4. For the best fit, measure your feet _____ you are standing up.

           where   when   why

Read the bold words and their meanings.

heroic	very brave
attempt	to make an effort; to try
communicate	to share information

Circle a word in each sentence that has a meaning *similar* to the underlined word.

1. Firefighters are brave because of the <u>heroic</u> ways they save people.

2. My little brother tries not to fall when he <u>attempts</u> to ride his bike.

3. I always tell my parents about my day at school, because I know it's important to <u>communicate</u>.

Write a paragraph using at least two of the pairs of *similar* words.

4. _____

_____

_____

_____

_____

Write the sentences correctly.

1. Last year on mine Birthday, I told my mom that I wanted to get a pet snake

_____

2. Even though she knowed how bad I wanted a snake, her still said no.

_____

Write the prepositional phrase to complete the sentence.

3. When Mom was little, a snake _____ crawled up her leg.

  slowly   at a pet shop   named Pete

Use context clues to figure out the meaning of the bold word. Then write the meaning on the line.

4. I don't think snakes are scary, but I don't want a pet that **frightens** my mom.

_____

Write the sentences correctly.

1. I can't wait to visit my friend on Saturday April 5.

_____

2. My friend lives on a farm when there are lots of geeses.

_____

Write the word that best completes the sentence.

3. Sometimes the geese chase us and we _____ to the barn.

  jog   skip   run

Use context clues to figure out the meaning of the bold word. Then write the meaning on the line.

4. One time I was **injured** when I fell on some rocks and scraped my knee.

_____

Write the sentences correctly.

1. Our class are doing a play called <u>all my friends have four legs</u>.

_____

2. My teacher, mrs. brown, asked me to be one of the main character's.

_____

Add punctuation to the sentence.

3. I am glad you asked me I said to Mrs. Brown I would love to be in the play

Write the word that correctly completes the complex sentence.

4. _____ I got my costume, I was surprised to see a bunny suit.

Where   When   Why

Write the sentences correctly.

1. At gatorland in Orlando Florida, you can learn how to trane a alligator.

_____

2. If you vizit Dinosaur World in Cave City Kentucky, you can digs for fossils.

_____

Write the missing word.

3. At the goat museum in Oregon, you _____ learn all about goats.

may   must   can

Write the word that best completes the sentence.

4. It is fun to _____ new and exciting places when you travel.

discover   view   notice

Read the bold homophones and their meanings.

cent	a coin; a penny
scent	a smell
sent	the past tense of *to send*

Write the homophone that best completes each sentence.

1. Mom's new perfume has the _____ of roses.

2. I bought a shirt online, but I _____ it back because it didn't fit.

3. My little brother has one dollar and one _____ in his piggy bank.

Write a paragraph using all three homophones.

4. _____

_____

_____

_____

_____

_____

Write the sentences correctly.

1. Lions is big cats who are best known for their loud rore.

_____

2. Did you know that a lion can be heared from five miles away

_____

Rewrite the sentences to make a compound sentence. Use the word _because_.

3. Sometimes people capture lions. People want to save lions from harm.

_____

Use context clues to figure out the meaning of the bold word. Then write the meaning on the line.

4. The lions that are kept in the zoo are in **captivity**.

_____

Write the sentences correctly.

1. I axed my dad if they would let me start a pet-sitting business?

_____

2. My dad sayed me could start a business if i gotted good grades.

_____

Identify the part of speech of the bold word. Explain what the word does in the sentence.

3. My mom **nicely** said that I would have to work very hard.

Part of speech: _____

Explain: _____

Complete the sentence with the comparative adverb.

4. Dad said that I would have to work _____ than ever before.

harder   hardest

Write the sentences correctly.

1. You will take well pitchers if you no how to use an camera.

_____

2. If you practise much, you'll soon be a well photographer.

_____

Rewrite the underlined part to put the words in the correct order.

3. If you have a <u>digital modern camera</u>, be sure to read the instruction manual.

_____

Draw a line between the prefix and the root word of the underlined word. Then write the meaning on the line.

4. A digital camera is handy because it lets you <u>preview</u> your pictures.

_____

Write the sentences correctly.

1. for a class projekt, I writed a letter to the famous person.

_____

2. I picked me a person who is very importent to the united states

_____

Write the words that correctly complete the sentence.

3. The person _____ I wrote a letter is Barack Obama.

        to who   to whom

Add punctuation to the sentence.

4. The first sentence of my letter said I am very proud to write to a U.S. president

Read the prepositions.

around	under	beside
over	on	across

Write the preposition that best completes each sentence.

1. I rode my bike _____ the block.

2. My best friend sits _____ from me in class.

3. Will you sit _____ me during the concert?

Write a paragraph using at least three of the prepositions from the box.

4. _____

_____

_____

_____

_____

_____

Write the sentences correctly.

1. Everybody in my family like to lissen at music

_____

2. My parents favoritest kind of music is jazz.

_____

Rewrite the sentences to make a compound sentence. Use a comma and the word _but_.

3. My sister and I stream music. Mom and Dad listen to CDs.

_____

Circle the meaning of the bold word.

4. Mom and Dad play CDs and sing loudly into a **microphone**.

   a. a machine that makes sounds louder

   b. a machine that lets you see objects up close

Write the sentences correctly.

1. Weet is one of the importanest crops in the World.

_____

2. Their is seven main kinds of potatos that grew in the united states.

_____

Write the missing words.

3. Lettuce grows well in _____ tomatoes grow well when it's hot.

      winter, but   winter but

Rewrite the underlined part to put the words in the correct order.

4. Spinach is a green leafy vegetable that can be planted in spring, fall, and winter.

_____

Write the sentences correctly.

1. Did you no that there are a difference between bugs and insects

_____

2. While bugs mouths work like a straw, insects chew they food.

_____

Complete the bold word with the suffix that means _can be done_.

3. Insects have **mov**_____ mouth parts, but bugs' mouths don't move.

       able   ment   ing

Circle the meaning of the bold word.

4. Another difference between them is that bugs have three **stages** of life, and most insects have four.

     a. steps in a process   b. raised floors or platforms

Write the sentences correctly.

1. A man on TV said that its raining cats and dogs so I runned outside to look.

_____

2. My sister said, "it cant really rain cats and dogs but once it rains frogs in england."

_____

Explain what the underlined idiom means.

3. I don't know if it can rain frogs, but once when I tried to sing, I had a <u>frog in my throat</u>.

_____

Complete the analogy.

4. rain : weather :: dog : _____

Read the bold idioms and their meanings.

Idiom	Meaning
hit the sack	to go to bed or to sleep
pulling your leg	playing a joke on someone
let the cat out of the bag	to share a secret

Write the idiom that best completes each sentence.

1. When I said there's a bug in your hair, I was _____.

2. The party is a surprise. Please don't _____.

3. You have to get up early, so you'd better _____.

Write a paragraph using two idioms from the box.

4. _____

_____

_____

_____

_____

_____

Write the sentences correctly.

1. People who sets a world record do something more better then anyone else.

_____

2. If a person sets a world record, their name could be in the book <u>guinness world records</u>.

_____

Write the word or words that best complete the sentence.

3. In 2010, the _____ drummer in a band was only five years old.

    most young   younger   youngest

Use context clues to figure out the meaning of the bold word. Then write the meaning on the line.

4. I like bubble gum so much, I think I will **attempt** to blow the most bubbles.

_____

Write the sentences correctly.

1. At school, me and my friends picks up trash we find laying on the ground.

_____

2. Litter is a big problum because it makes the school look badly.

_____

Write the word or words that best complete the sentence.

3. Littering is bad for people and even _____ for the planet.

    badder   more worser   worse

Add punctuation to the sentence.

4. I made a flier that said Litter is not cool Please don't pollute our school

Write the sentences correctly.

1. If you wants to make a memory box, you needed string glue markers and a box.

_____

2. Youll also need a few pieces of tissue paper to deckorate the box.

_____

Use context clues to figure out the meaning of the bold word. Then write the meaning on the line.

3. A memory box is a good place to **store** your photos and other items you want to save.

_____

Write the suffix that correctly completes the bold word.

4. Looking at old photos can be **real**_____ fun.

y   ly

Write the sentences correctly.

1. On september 9 1850, California becomes a U.S. state.

_____

2. Today, the citys in California that had the mostest people is Los Angeles and San Diego.

_____

Write the word that best completes the sentence.

3. Many pioneers _____ in California when gold was found.

stayed   settled   lived

The Latin root *vid* means "to see." Circle the meaning of the underlined word.

4. At school we saw a <u>video</u> about the Gold Rush.

a. a program you hear on the radio   b. a program you watch on a TV or computer

Read the bold word roots and their meanings.

port	to carry
mot	to move
loc	place

Complete each bold word with a root from the box.

1. Can you tell me the _____**ation** of the ice-cream store?

2. People use camels for **trans**_____**ation** through the desert.

3. The _____**or** in Dad's car isn't working, so we can't go anywhere.

Write a paragraph using two of the words you made. Then circle the roots.

4. _____

_____

_____

_____

_____

_____

Write the sentences correctly.

1. When the children ran thru the house, they was shout loudly.

_____

2. The childrens' babysitter said, "Stop! You must slow down and play quiet"

_____

Write the missing word.

3. "The children _____ disobey me may not watch TV," she said.

                that   who   which

Complete the bold word with the prefix that means _completely_.

4. The children were _____**joyed** when the babysitter said they could watch TV.

         over   non   under

Write the sentences correctly.

1. Appleton Wisconsin, is the sity when I used to live.

_____

2. We moved, because my Dad getted a new job.

_____

Write the word that correctly completes the sentence.

3. Green Bay is the city _____ we live now.

                which   that   where

What is wrong with the sentence? Circle the answer.

4. I like Green Bay, I like Appleton better.

     a. run-on sentence   b. sentence fragment

Write the sentences correctly.

1. I seen a poster at school that said "enter the school writing contest."

_____

2. I writed a story about an elephunt that can draw and paint

_____

Use context clues to figure out the meaning of the bold word. Then write the meaning on the line.

3. A lot of students entered the contest to **compete** for first prize.

_____

Draw a line between the root word and the suffix of the underlined word. Then write the meaning on the line.

4. My story won the contest, and I got a prize for Best <u>Writer</u>.

_____

Write the sentences correctly.

1. Before there was tranes, mens and womens rided horses or walked.

_____

2. People wanted to move more fast so they invent trains that move on tracks.

_____

Circle the meaning of the bold word root.

3. My favorite ride at the park is the loco**mot**ive because it goes fast.

a. to pedal   b. to move   c. to push

Make the word *speedy* a comparative adverb.

4. The train is fast, but the roller coaster is even _____.

speedy

Read the bold word and its different meanings.

> **light**   a. to cause to give off light
>   b. a lamp that gives off light
>   c. having little weight; not heavy

Which meaning of *light* is used in the sentence? Write the letter on the line.

1. My backpack is easy to carry because it is so light.   _____

2. Before you cut the birthday cake, I need to light the candles.   _____

3. Please turn off the light when you leave the room.   _____

Write a paragraph using two of the meanings of the word *light*.

4. _____

_____

_____

_____

_____

Write the sentences correctly.

1. One of the popularest pets in america is tropical fishes.

   _____

2. If you want pet fish, you have to buy aquarium food and deckorations.

   _____

Identify the part of speech of the bold words. Explain what the words do in the sentence.

3. My aquarium has **colored** rocks, **plastic** plants, and a **treasure** chest.

   Part of speech: _____

   Explain: _____

Use context clues to figure out the meaning of the bold word. Then write the meaning on the line.

4. When you first buy an aquarium, you have to **assemble** all of the parts and pieces.

   _____

Write the sentences correctly.

1. They're are many facts about Camels but some things people believe are not true.

   _____

2. Camels do has curlee eyelashes but they no have water in its humps.

   _____

Write the word that best completes the sentence.

3. Some people think camels are _____ because they spit and groan.

                  ugly   dirty   unpleasant

Write the missing word.

4. Camels work hard for people, but camels _____ also hurt people.

                  must   should   could

Write the sentences correctly.

1. Its a well idea to save your money so you can bye something you realy want.

_____

2. If you is a kid who wants to save money, you should get some piggy bank.

_____

Underline the prepositional phrases in this sentence.

3. After school, I'm walking to the bank that is near the mall.

Explain what the underlined expression means.

4. I <u>felt like a million dollars</u> when I bought myself a baseball cap.

_____

Write the sentences correctly.

1. I like getting in girl scouts because we do lots of fun activitys.

_____

2. The very first groop of scouts gotted together on March 12 1912.

_____

Write the noun that best completes the sentence.

3. When girls join the group, they make the Girl Scout _____.

                                                                               uniform   Promise   cookies

Underline the part of the sentence that shows someone's exact written words.

4. The Girl Scout website says that "girls discover fun and friendship."

Read the bold word and its different meanings.

> state   a. the condition of a person or thing
>   b. any of the places that make up a country
>   c. to express in words

Which meaning of *state* is used in the sentence? Write the letter on the line.

1. I was born in the state of Virginia, but now I live in California.   _____

2. The principal stated that there will be an assembly on Friday.   _____

3. I was in a state of happiness when I got an A⁺ on my test.   _____

Write a paragraph using at least two different meanings of the word *state*.

4. _____

_____

_____

_____

_____

_____

Write the sentences correctly.

1. On the first day of school, mine friends and me walked to school together.

_____

2. Because I wear a new pair of shoes, my foots hurted and it was hard to walk.

_____

Write the word that best completes the sentence.

3. I was _____ when I tripped and fell in front of everyone.

    worried   sad   embarrassed

Explain what the underlined expression means.

4. I felt as helpless as a baby when I was lying on the ground.

_____

_____

Write the sentences correctly.

1. There is many ways for people to travul if them want to go somewhere.

_____

2. In london england, people ride on red tall busses.

_____

Rewrite the sentences to make one sentence.

3. Some people use animals to go places. They ride horses, elephants, and camels.

_____

Draw a line between the prefix and the root word of the underlined word. Then write the meaning on the line.

4. School buses transport hundreds of school children each day.

_____

Write the sentences correctly.

1. "Mom, can we go at the libary and check out some books." I asked.

_____

2. Mom sayed "Yes, but you half to get ready quick, because it closes soon"

_____

Use context clues to figure out the meaning of the bold word. Then write the meaning on the line.

3. When we got to the library, Mom told me to ask the **librarian** for my own library card.

_____

The Latin root _sign_ means "to mark." Complete the sentence with the word that has the root _sign_.

4. The librarian gave me a piece of paper and asked me to write my

_____ on the line.

age   signature   weight

Write the sentences correctly.

1. Cuckoo byrds eat insects and its favorite type of food is the harry caterpillar.

_____

2. The commonest bird on earth is the Chicken.

_____

Draw a line between the root word and the suffix of the underlined word. Then write the meaning on the line.

3. Penguins are birds that have short legs and are flightless.

_____

Write the word that best completes the sentence.

4. Some types of birds are so _____ that they can make and use tools.

able   sly   smart

Read the paragraph. Use context clues to figure out the meaning of the underlined words.

> I broke my leg when I fell off my skateboard.
> It was very <u>painful</u>. Today I am <u>nervous</u>
> because I am going to the doctor. But I am also
> <u>cheerful</u> because Mom bought me a bunch of
> balloons with smiley faces on them.

Write the word that best completes the sentence. Use an underlined word from above.

1. I am not shy, but I get _____ when I have to speak in class.

2. Pulling out your own tooth can be _____.

3. When I woke up this morning, Mom said, "Good morning, Sunshine."

   Mom is always so _____.

Write the definition of each word.

4. painful:

   _____

   nervous:

   _____

   cheerful:

   _____

Write the sentences correctly.

1. If you need some thing to do this summer, think about help the comunity.

_____

2. You could pick up trash on the beech, or mow lawns in you nayborhood.

_____

Write the correct form of the date.

3. Make a Difference Day is _____.

       october 22 2016   October 22, 2016   October, 22 2016

Explain what the underlined expression means.

4. The man who is painting the community center asked me to <u>lend him a hand</u>.

_____

Write the sentences correctly.

1. Next time you eat you vegetables, think about what you is eating.

_____

2. Plants has lots of diffrent parts which we can eat.

_____

Add punctuation to the sentence.

3. The parts of plants that we can eat include roots stems leaves and seeds

Write the word that correctly completes the sentence.

4. Did you know that you are eating the stem of a plant _____ you eat asparagus?

    why   where   when

Write the sentences correctly.

1. If you wants to laff, you should read a book call <u>the big joke book</u>.

_____

2. When I readed a book, I was laugh so hard that I was near crying.

_____

Circle the meaning of the underlined adage.

3. Whenever I'm upset, Mom says that <u>laughter is the best medicine</u>.

  a. You should take medicine when you're upset.   b. Laughter makes you feel good.

Make the words *long* and *loud* comparative adverbs.

4. The _____ and _____ you laugh, the better you'll feel.
       long   loud

Write the sentences correctly.

1. My family don't have the cellphone like many peoples families do.

_____

2. Our phone have a long cord and we can't go outside to talk.

_____

Draw a line between the prefix and the root word of the underlined word. Then write the meaning on the line.

3. I <u>dislike</u> our phone, but it works just fine.

_____

Circle the meaning of the bold word.

4. Dad said I can have a cellphone when I can help pay the **bill**.

  a. a bird's beak   b. a piece of paper money   c. a printed list of money a person owes

Read the words.

similar   job   get

hide   show   give

Use the words from the box to write a synonym next to each word.

1. acquire _____   conceal _____

demonstrate _____   contribute _____

related _____   function _____

Complete each sentence using the synonym pairs you just made.

2. My big brother wants to _____ a new skateboard, but first he has

to _____ the money.

3. If you _____ me how to make pancakes, I will

_____ how to make pie.

4. To help homeless animals, some people _____ blankets

to the animal shelter, and some people _____ money.

Write the sentences correctly.

1. summer vacashun is a time when me and my sisters does many fun things.

_____

2. We go to Space camp or we learn to play an sport like tennis.

_____

Write the adjectives in the correct order.

3. Sometimes we fly _____ kites at the beach.

        bright big   big bright

Explain what the underlined simile means.

4. I feel <u>as free as a bird</u> when I run across the wet sand.

_____

Write the sentences correctly.

1. Walt Disney was born on December 5 1901 in Hermosa Illinois.

_____

2. Maybe you have saw Mickey Mouse or Goofy on your vacation to disneyland.

_____

Write the word that best completes the sentence.

3. Children like to hug the characters because they are so _____.

        lovable   agreeable

Write the word that means _to play again_. Use the prefix _re_.

4. If you make a video of your trip, you can _____ it over and over.

Write the sentences correctly.

1. Twins are too children that is born together.

_____

2. Some twins look exact alike, but are very different in other ways.

_____

Write the word that means the opposite of the bold word.

3. One twin could be **tall**, and the other twin could be _____.

Write the word that means _not possible_. Use the prefix _im_.

4. Sometimes it is _____ to tell twins apart.

Write the sentences correctly.

1. The twin boys in my class invited me to his Birthday partie.

_____

2. One of the boys are my best friend so I couldnt wait to go.

_____

Write the missing word.

3. I heard that there _____ be a petting zoo at the party.

           must   might   should

Draw a line between the root word and the suffix of the underlined word. Then write the meaning on the line.

4. I am <u>hopeful</u> that I will get to see some cute goats.

_____

Read the bold word roots and their meanings.

act	to do
vis	to see
ped	foot

Complete each bold word with a root from the box.

1. People who walk places must be careful when they cross the street.

   Drivers must stop to let the _____**estrians** cross safely.

2. In the movie *Spy Kids*, two children rescue their parents and save the world.

   The movie has a lot of _____**ion**!

3. Cats can see well at night. Their excellent _____**ion** helps them catch their food.

Write a paragraph using two of the words you made. Then circle the roots.

4. _____

   _____

   _____

   _____

   _____

   _____

Write the sentences correctly.

1. Pluto was once knowed as the smaller Planet in a solar system.

_____

2. In august 2006, scientists said that Pluto is to small to be a planet.

_____

Write the root that correctly completes the bold word. Use the word _see_ as a clue.

3. You can only see Pluto with a **tele**_____.

                     phone   graph   scope

Write a synonym for the bold word.

4. The best way to **see** Pluto is to _____ it through the Hubble Space Telescope.

Write the sentences correctly.

1. The invention that is the more famous is the weel.

_____

2. The telefone car and electric light bulb was also inportant inventions.

_____

Complete the analogy.

3. create : creative :: invent : _____

Use context clues to figure out the meaning of the bold word. Then write the meaning on the line.

4. There is nothing else like the Pet Rock, and that makes it **unique**.

_____

Write the sentences correctly.

1. Desserts are dry places that don't recieve many rain.

_____

2. Desert Animals gets their water from food, and store the water in their bodys.

_____

Use context clues to figure out the meaning of the bold word. Then write the meaning on the line.

3. Only a few kinds of animals can **survive** without water and without much food.

_____

Write a complete sentence. Begin the sentence with the words *even if*.

4. it doesn't have water, the kangaroo rat can survive in the desert.

_____

Write the sentences correctly.

1. You doesn't need a lot of ekwipment to go fishing.

_____

2. You does need a fishing pole to catch them fishes.

_____

Write the word or words that best complete the sentence.

3. There is a law that you need a _____ to fish for some types of fish.

    note   permission slip   license

Circle the meaning of the bold word.

4. Kids who fish have to be **patient** because they have to wait for the fish to bite.

    a. a person getting medical care from a doctor   b. calm, self-controlled

Read the bold words and their similar meanings.

donate	to give for a good cause
give	to make a present of
lend	to give for temporary use

Choose the word that best completes each sentence.

1. I will _____ you my jacket, but I need it back after school.

    lend   give

2. Mom said I could _____ some of my clothes to the homeless shelter.

        donate   lend

3. I wonder what my parents will _____ me for my birthday.

            give   lend

Write a paragraph using two of the words from the box.

4. _____

    _____

    _____

    _____

    _____

    _____

Write the sentences correctly.

1. A girl in my class named anna told me about their pogo stick.

_____

2. Anna said, "If youd like to, you may jump on it, but don't hurt herself."

_____

Complete the sentence with the word that is most precise.

3. To jump without falling, I had to _____ on the pogo stick.

                         stay   balance

Underline another word for *hopeful*.

4. I was encouraged when I jumped three times in a row!

Write the sentences correctly.

1. Menny poems rhyme but there are no rules for writeing poems.

_____

2. Once I red a book that's called this poem doesn't rhyme.

_____

Circle the relative adverb.

3. I read poems when I want to feel good.

Complete the sentence with the word or words that are most precise.

4. When I read poems about birds, I can _____ what it's like to fly.

                      imagine   think of

Write the sentences correctly.

1. If you could chews where you live, wood you live near a farm city or beach.

   _____

2. Some people think that the beach was the better place of all to live.

   _____

Complete the sentence with a word that means _full of peace_.

3. I would like to live in the country because it is quiet and _____.

Complete the sentence with the superlative adjective.

4. I don't like to live in the city because it is the _____ of all places.

   noisier   noisiest

Write the sentences correctly.

1. Pizza is made most of bread cheese and sauce.

   _____

2. Many people bake pizza in our oven, and eat it when it's hot.

   _____

Write the missing word.

3. People _____ also have pizza delivered.

   must   should   can

Underline the part of the sentence that can stand on its own. Circle the part that _cannot_ stand on its own.

4. Although pizza is tasty, it's not healthful to eat too much pizza.

Read each type of expression and its definition.

simile	compares two different things using *like* or *as*
metaphor	compares two different things without using *like* or *as*

Read each sentence. Then write *simile* or *metaphor* to describe the bold words.

1. My grandma drives **as slow as a snail**. _____

2. The duck's **feathers are silk**. _____

3. I slept **like a log**. _____

Write a paragraph using one simile or one metaphor from above.

4. _____

_____

_____

_____

_____

_____

Write the sentences correctly.

1. Dogs are knowed as a humans' best friend but cats can be as friendly as dogs.

_____

2. In mine opinion, people doesn't understand cats.

_____

Write the word or words that best complete the sentence.

3. You might think cats are unfriendly because they _____.

like to sleep   like to be alone   cry

Explain the meaning of the bold simile.

4. Cats and dogs are **like night and day**, but they both can be friendly.

_____

Write the sentences correctly.

1. Noah Webster was a teecher whom made it easyer for students to learn to spell.

_____

2. In early america, people spellt words in many different ways.

_____

Write the adjectives in the correct order.

3. Mr. Webster wanted there to be _____ dictionary.

American one   one American

Write a synonym for the bold word.

4. Webster's dictionary had new and **simple** spellings. _____

Write the sentences correctly.

1. The food, that astronauts eat today, is much better than it use to be.

_____

2. The first Space food comed in tubes and look like baby food.

_____

Rewrite the sentence to make two sentences.

3. Today, space food is tasty, and the food is also healthful.

_____

Write a pronoun to replace the bold word. Explain how the pronoun makes the sentence better.

4. Astronauts get to choose their food before **astronauts** travel into space.

Pronoun: _____

Explain: _____

Write the sentences correctly.

1. Recycleing trash is won way to keep planit Earth healthy.

_____

2. Maybe you has heard the saying "reduce, reuse, recycle".

_____

Use context clues to figure out the meaning of the bold word. Then write the meaning on the line.

3. If you want to help **reduce** the trash in the world, don't throw stuff away!

_____

Complete the sentence with the word or words that are most precise.

4. The environment makes life possible for us, so we must _____ it.

care about   protect   help

Read the pair of nouns in each row.

regular nouns (person, place, or thing)	abstract nouns (cannot see, hear, smell, touch, or taste)
spaceship	dream
child	fear
president	honesty

Complete each sentence with a pair of nouns from above.

1. One famous _____ was known for his _____.

2. I had a _____ about flying in a _____.

3. When I was a _____, I had a _____ of the dark.

Write two abstract nouns.

4. _____   _____

Write the sentences correctly.

1. Has you ever played a card game call "Go Fish?"

_____

2. Yesterday, i tryed it for the first time and now it's a favorite game of his.

_____

Write the words that form the present progressive verb tense.

3. In this card game, two players _____ turns fishing
   and catching.   are taking   were taking   will be taking

Add punctuation to the sentence.

4. The first player asks Do you have any kings The second player says Go fish

Write the sentences correctly.

1. Cave peoples was the first Humans to kreate art.

_____

2. They painted animuls on the walls of caves but no one really nose why.

_____

Write the best word to complete the sentence.

3. We will probably never be able to _____ what the art means.
                              prove   show   tell

Draw a line between the root word and the suffix of the underlined word. Then write the meaning on the line.

4. We do know that cave people were great <u>artists</u>.

_____

Write the sentences correctly.

1. Fire works was invented more then two thousand years ago.

_____

2. People think that marco polo brung fireworks with him from china.

_____

Use context clues to figure out the meaning of the bold word. Then write the meaning on the line.

3. At first, the only colors that people could **produce** were orange and white.

_____

Write the word or words that correctly complete the sentence.

4. Orange fireworks are _____ to make than blue fireworks.

      easy   more easy   easier

Write the sentences correctly.

1. If you has a dog that acts real bad, you can take him to a school for dogs.

_____

2. You dog will quick learn how to act nice and obey you.

_____

Complete the bold word with the prefix that means *not* or *opposite from*.

3. If your dog _____**obeys** you, do not get angry with him.

      re   dis   un

The word *operate* means "to work." The root *co* means "with" or "together." What is the meaning of the bold word?

4. Be patient and your dog will learn to **cooperate** with you and follow your commands.

_____

Read the bold words and their meanings.

fragile	easily broken
descend	to move or fall downward
sensible	showing good judgment

Circle a word in each sentence that means the *opposite* of the underlined word.

1. Although the flower pot is <u>fragile</u>, it is sturdy enough to hold a small plant.

2. The plane will ascend higher and higher, and then it will slowly <u>descend</u> from the sky.

3. A <u>sensible</u> person saves his or her money, but a foolish person spends it on junk.

Write the definition of each word.

4. sturdy:

_____

ascend:

_____

foolish:

_____

Write the sentences correctly.

1. Did you here that opposite day is on january 25 2016?

_____

2. At much schools, there is a lot of sillyness on this day.

_____

Rewrite the sentences to make a complex sentence. Begin the sentence with _while_.

3. Some kids wear their clothes backward. Some kids eat breakfast for lunch.

_____

Write a word that means the opposite of the bold word.

4. I think Opposite Day is **boring**.   _____

Write the sentences correctly.

1. Female owls are larger and heavyer than mail owls.

_____

2. Owls' have sharp beaks and claws to help it catch and eat its food.

_____

Write the adjectives in the correct order.

3. _____ owls are called snowy owls.

    Large white   White large

Write the missing word.

4. If you'd like to see a snowy owl, you _____ watch a _Harry Potter_ movie.

                should   may   will

Write the sentences correctly.

1. The Pilgrims sailed above the Atlantic ocean on a ship called the <u>mayflower</u>.

_____

2. The Pilgrims spended two months at see before they spoted land.

_____

Use context clues to figure out the meaning of the bold word. Then write the meaning on the line.

3. The Pilgrims **endured** storms, sickness, and a cold winter to get to America.

_____

Write the words that best complete the sentence.

4. The worst thing I have endured is _____.

    watching TV   getting a tooth pulled   reading a book

Write the sentences correctly.

1. On mount rushmore, four U.S. president's heads are carved in rock.

_____

2. The closer city to these monument is Keystone South Dakota.

_____

Circle the meaning of the bold word.

3. The man who made Mount Rushmore wanted to **draw** lots of people to his state.

    a. to make a picture   b. to cause people to come to a place

Complete the analogy.

4. rock : solid :: water : _____

Read the words.

> automatic   uncertain   deny
>
> infrequent   compare   concealed

Use the words from the box to write an antonym next to each word.

1. contrast _____   manual   _____

    confirm _____   convinced _____

    revealed _____   constant _____

Complete each sentence using the antonym pairs you just made.

2. The pirate _____ that he found treasure, but he

    _____ the hiding place.

3. Freezing temperatures are _____ in my town, and hot weather

    is _____.

4. I'm _____ about where my new friend lives, but I'm

    _____ that we live near each other.

Write the sentences correctly.

1. If you wanna know about your home state, theres a websight you can go to.

   _____

2. On the page called student state facts, I finded out mine states nickname and bird.

   _____

Complete the sentence with the superlative form of the adjective *large*.

3. In my home state of Iowa, the _____ city is Des Moines.

   larger   largest

Rewrite the sentences to make a complex sentence. Begin the sentence with the word *although*.

4. Des Moines is the capital of Iowa. The first capital of Iowa was Iowa City.

   _____

Write the sentences correctly.

1. Has you read the book <u>alice's adventures in wonderland</u>?

   _____

2. The tail begins where Alice sees a rabbit who is wearing a coat and look at the watch.

   _____

   _____

Add punctuation to the sentence.

3. Oh my ears and whiskers, how late it's getting! says the rabbit.

Complete the sentence with a prepositional phrase. Then circle the preposition.

4. Alice follows the White Rabbit _____.

   down a rabbit hole   because he is cute

Write the sentences correctly.

1. I think salsa is one of the yummyest foods there are.

   _____

2. The bestest salsa is maked with tomatoes onions peppers and spices.

   _____

Write the best word to complete the sentence.

3. The salsa I like is so hot and spicy, I have to _____ lots of water
   when I eat it.   sip   gulp   drink

Complete the sentence with the word that has the correct spelling.

4. I wonder if there are any foods that are _____ than salsa.

   spicyer   spicier

Write the sentences correctly.

1. My Mom is a cooker at a restaurant called time to dine.

   _____

2. Mom buys the fresher ingredients she can find so the food is delishus.

   _____

Write the word that correctly completes the sentence.

3. Mom _____ the ingredients before she cooks the food.
   prepares   fixes

Use context clues to figure out the meaning of the bold word. Then write the meaning on the line.

4. When Mom is really busy, I **assist** her by washing dishes.

   _____

Read the bold word roots and their meanings.

graph	to write or draw
tele	distant
scope	to watch or see

Complete each bold word with a root from the box.

1. My grandma lives far away, so we have to talk on the _____**phone**.

2. The bug is so tiny that I have to use a **micro**_____ to see it.

3. When I broke my leg, my teacher signed her **auto**_____ on my cast.

Write a paragraph using two of the words you made. Then circle the roots.

4. _____

_____

_____

_____

_____

_____

Write the sentences correctly.

1. Birds has small brains compared to ours but they is smart than you think.

_____

2. Birds know that the most better time to catch worms is before the son comes up.

_____

Draw a line between the root word and the suffix of the underlined word. Then write the meaning on the line.

3. The birds that are early will be the most <u>successful</u> at finding worms.

_____

Explain the meaning of the underlined proverb.

4. This morning I got to school early because <u>the early bird gets the worm</u>!

_____

Write the sentences correctly.

1. Did you no that do something nice day is in October 5.

_____

2. The two easyest things to do is smiled at someone and say hi.

_____

Complete the sentence with the words that are related to the bold word.

3. One way to be **thoughtful** is to _____.

                                watch TV   take out the trash

Circle the meaning of the bold word.

4. When you help people, you are showing them an **act** of kindness.

     a. a thing done; a deed   b. to perform in a play or movie

Write the sentences correctly.

1. Some animals make sounds which wood surprize you.

_____

2. Wolfs cry like a baby geeses honk like a horn and cats purr like the motor of a car.

_____

_____

Write a complete sentence to fix the sentence fragment.

3. Many other animals that make funny sounds.

_____

Write the two things that are being compared in the simile.

4. I think that a hippo sounds like a hungry stomach.

_____

Write the sentences correctly.

1. We're finaly inside the National Museum Of American History in Washington DC.

_____

2. I can't wate to see the very first flag but my sister wants to see oscar the grouch first.

_____

Write the best word to complete the sentence.

3. "Wow! There's Abraham Lincoln's hat," I _____.

whisper   say   exclaim

**Draw lines between the prefix, the root word, and the suffix of the underlined word.
Then write the meaning on the line.**

4. "That's interesting," Dad says, "but this covered wagon is <u>unbelievable</u>!"

_____

Read the bold phrase and its different meanings.

> **pick up**   a. to lift an object or a person
>   b. to make tidy
>   c. to gather together

Which meaning of the phrase _pick up_ is used in the sentence? Write the letter on the line.

1. Please pick up your room before you leave for school.   _____

2. She picked up the pieces of the puzzle.   _____

3. I picked up my sister and gave her a hug.   _____

Write a paragraph using at least two of the meanings of the phrase _pick up_.

4. _____

_____

_____

_____

_____

_____

Write the sentences correctly.

1. Snakes are finded near everywhere in the World except antarctica.

_____

2. Some snakes live in the see some live underground and some clime trees.

_____

Rewrite the sentence so it is not a run-on sentence.

3. Snakes' tongues are useful they help snakes feel and smell.

_____

Circle the two words that mean almost the same thing. Then write *synonyms* or *antonyms* on the line.

4. A snake is always looking for food or enemies, so its tongue is constantly moving.

_____

Write the sentences correctly.

1. Maybe you doesn't chew gum but the ancient greeks does.

_____

2. Chewing gum come from trees and is one of the older candies in the world.

_____

Write the adjectives in the correct order.

3. An American inventor turned tree sap into _____ pieces of gum.

                 rubbery small small rubbery

Complete the sentence with an antonym for the bold word.

4. Gum that is made today has **natural** and _____ ingredients.

Write the sentences correctly.

1. Humpback wales are knowed for there singing.

_____

2. Scientists don't realy know why whales sing or what its songs mean.

_____

Complete the sentence with the word that has the correct spelling.

3. The humpback whale is the _____ whale when it comes to singing.

                 noisiest   noisyest

Draw a line between the root word and the suffix of the underlined word. Then write the meaning on the line.

4. When a male whale is singing, it floats in the water <u>motionless</u>.

_____

Write the sentences correctly.

1. I like to play the bored game called monopoly.

_____

2. My friends favorite game to play is checkers and tic-tac-toe.

_____

Write the words that form the past progressive verb tense.

3. Yesterday, my friend and I _____ checkers.

       are playing   were playing   will be playing

Underline the verbs in the sentence. Explain what the verbs do in the sentence.

4. My cat jumped up and knocked the game board over, so we decided to play outside.

Explain: _____

Read each type of expression and its definition.

adage	a popular old saying that people believe is true **example: When it rains it pours.**
idiom	an expression that means something different from what it seems to mean **example: I'm all ears.**
proverb	a wise old saying that gives advice or teaches a lesson **example: Practice makes perfect.**

Write *adage, idiom,* or *proverb* to name the type of expression.

1. I'm all ears. _____

    Practice makes perfect. _____

    When it rains it pours. _____

Write the expression that goes with each sentence.

2. Dad said that he had a funny story to tell me.

    I said, "_____."

3. I told my mom that I didn't feel like practicing the piano.

    My mom said, "_____."

4. Today I woke up late, I missed the bus, and I forgot my books.

    I said to myself, "_____."

Write the sentences correctly.

1. uncle james offerd to took me to the baseball game.

_____

2. I thank my uncle, but told he that I had to do chores before I can go.

_____

Write the missing word.

3. "I think I am going to the game, but I _____ be late," I told him.

might   can   should

Underline the proverb in the sentence. Then explain what the proverb means.

4. "I hope you can get there on time, but better late than never," my uncle said.

_____

Write the sentences correctly.

1. Oranges is a juicey citrus fruit that has a lot of Vitamin c.

_____

2. Oranges grows in trees in warm, tropical places such as spain.

_____

Rewrite the sentences to make one sentence.

3. Columbus brought the first orange seeds to the New World. He brought them in 1493.

_____

Make the word *healthy* a superlative adjective.

4. Some people think that oranges are the _____ food there is.

healthy

Write the sentences correctly.

1. One of the mane jobs of the nose are to help us smell.

   _____

2. The Human nose can smell different many oders.

   _____

Rewrite the sentences to make one complex sentence. Begin the sentence with the subordinating conjunction *before*.

3. Air goes into your lungs. Your nose warms the air.

   _____

Complete the analogy.

4. nose : smell :: lungs : _____

Write the sentences correctly.

1. Every country gots a flag as their national simbol.

   _____

2. Flags had many different feetures, including colors designs and writing.

   _____

Complete the sentence with the word that means the same as the prefix *tri*.

3. Many flags have a triangle on them. A triangle has _____ sides.

                                                            one   two   three

Complete the sentence with the correct relative pronoun.

4. A country _____ flag shows a red circle is Japan.

       whom   whose   who

Read the paragraph.

> I was glad when Mom said I could go to the movies. But she <u>stated</u> I had to clean my room before I could go. At first I argued that I didn't want to. But finally I grumbled that I would. Mom was delighted when I announced that my room was clean. She declared that I could go to the movies. I was so thrilled that I shouted "Hurray!"

Look at the paragraph in the box. Find more precise words for _said_. Write the words on the lines. The first one is done for you.

1. _____stated_____   _____   _____

_____   _____   _____

Rewrite each sentence. Replace the word _said_ with a more precise word from above.

2. "The spelling test will be tomorrow," my teacher **said**.

_____

When I fell down the stairs, I **said** "Help!"

_____

"I'm too tired to get out of bed," the boy **said**.

_____

Write a sentence using a word for _said_ from number 1.

3. _____

_____

Think of your own word for _said_ and write it on the line.

4. _____

Write the sentences correctly.

1. "My friends are comeing over for dinner tonite," my little sister said.

_____

2. "What are your friends favorite foods to eat," Mom asked.

_____

Add punctuation to the sentence.

3. My sister handed Mom a note that said We would like mud pie for dinner.

Circle the meaning of the bold word root.

4. When it was time to eat, I saw two empty chairs and my sister's in**vis**ible friends.

    a. to see   b. to move   c. to speak

Write the sentences correctly.

1. On August 5 2012, a space robot traveled to mars for a important mission.

_____

2. The rover named curiosity had cameras, so that we could see what mars look like.

_____

Complete the bold word with the suffix that means *the act of*.

3. When *Curiosity* landed on Mars, it was a great **achieve**_____.

                                          ness   ment   al

Circle the proper noun. Write the abstract noun on the line.

4. We watched with curiosity to see what *Curiosity* would find there.

    abstract noun: _____

Write the sentences correctly.

1. Your body do a lot of jobs to keep you helthy.

_____

2. When you are cold, your mussels move and that makes your body shivver.

_____

Complete the bold word with a suffix that means *the act of*.

3. When you shiver, the **move**_____ of your body warms you.

Write the adjectives in the correct order.

4. If you start shivering in _____ weather, you should go inside.

         freezing cold   cold freezing

Write the sentences correctly.

1. Hurricanes are majer storms that make waves wind and, rain.

_____

2. A storm isn't called a hurricane til the winds are moveing real fast.

_____

Complete the bold word with the suffix that means *in the manner of*.

3. Most of a hurricane is made up of **dangerous**_____ strong winds.

        ness   er   ly

Complete the sentence with the best word.

4. People can be prepared if they know when and _____ these storms will occur.

      where   while

Read the modal auxiliary verbs and what they tell about.

modal auxiliary verbs	tell about
can could	ability
may might could	possibility
must	obligation
should ought to	advice

Complete each sentence with a modal auxiliary verb from the category given.

1. You _____ take an umbrella with you because it's going to rain.
   advice

2. I _____ go to the movies but I'm not sure yet.
   possibility

3. We _____ remember to feed the dog before we leave for the day.
   obligation

4. They _____ beat the other team if they work together.
   ability

Write the sentences correctly.

1. The wolve is a member of the animal family that includes dogs, and foxxes.

_____

2. Too well-knowed types of wolfs is the gray wolf and the red wolf.

_____

Complete the sentence with the superlative form of the adjective.

3. The red wolf is the _____ of the wolves and is the most endangered.

    rare

Use context clues to figure out the meaning of the bold word. Then write the meaning on the line.

4. Gray wolves **occupy** many different places, but the places where they live have been reduced.

_____

Write the sentences correctly.

1. On March 2 1903, the golden poppy becomed the offisul flower of California.

_____

2. Some people beleive that the poppy is one of the beautifulest flowers in the world.

_____

Complete the sentence with the correct preposition. Then circle the prepositional phrase.

3. The man who named the flower saw golden hills when he sailed

_____ San Francisco Bay.

  between   throughout   into

Underline the metaphor. Write the two things that are being compared.

4. In Antelope Valley, California, the poppies are a sea of orange.

_____

Write the sentences correctly.

1. Wood you like to explore the temple of trash exhibit

_____

2. You should visit the trash museum at 211 Murphy Road in Hartford Connecticut.

_____

Complete the sentence with a synonym for *find*.

3. In the game "Where's the Rat?" you can try to _____ a rubber rat.

　　　　　　　　　　　　　　locate　　　　touch　　　　smell

Complete the sentence with the word that is the most precise.

4. At the viewing area, you can _____ people sorting trash.

　　　　　　　　　　　　see　　　　notice　　　　view

Write the sentences correctly.

1. Our schools soccer team is called the Gray Foxes because that's my state animal.

_____

2. The team wants their name changeed to the pink panthers.

_____

Rewrite the sentences to make a compound sentence. Use a comma and the coordinating conjunction *so*.

3. We wanted colorful uniforms. We chose a team name with the word "pink" in it.

_____

Write the words that form the future progressive verb tense.

4. I _____ to the principal to ask permission.

is writing　　　　　was writing　　　　　will be writing

Read the words that describe actions, emotions, and states of being.

actions	emotions	states of being
squealed	delighted	curious
urged	concerned	thoughtful
praised	pleased	proud

Write the word that best completes each sentence. Use a word from the category given.

1. The child _____ with joy when she saw her new bike.
   action

2. Please be home before dark, because I am _____ about your safety.
   emotion

3. I am so _____ of myself for helping Mom make dinner.
   state of being

Write a sentence using a word from one of the categories in the box.

4. _____

_____

Write the sentences correctly.

1. My granma and granpa has a farm where there are daley jobs to do.

_____

2. They make sure the animals had food water and a clean sleeping area.

_____

Use context clues to figure out the meaning of the bold word. Then write the meaning on the line.

3. Workers water the fields and **harvest** the crops that are ready to be picked.

_____

Circle the meaning of the bold word root.

4. A **tract**or is used to pull loads of crops across the fields.

    a. to see   b. to pull or drag   c. to break

Write the sentences correctly.

1. "I can do these puzzel more fast than you can," I said to my friend.

_____

2. "Lets race to see whom finishes first" my friend replyed.

_____

Complete the bold word with a prefix that means *not* or *the opposite of*.

3. My friend was _____**couraged** when he couldn't finish his puzzle.

    en   dis   re

Underline the adage in the sentence. Then explain what the adage means.

4. "I'll help you finish your puzzle, because two heads are better than one," I said.

_____

Write the sentences correctly.

1. Men has invented many things, such as car, the sewing mashine, and peanut butter.

   _____

2. Womans have invented many things, too but we've only herd about a few of them.

   _____

Use context clues to figure out the meaning of the bold word root. Then circle the meaning.

3. A woman invented **man**ual windshield wipers that drivers could pull with a handle.

   a. foot   b. measure   c. hand

Underline the word that means *to pull someone's attention away*. Then circle the part of the word that means *pull*.

4. Some people thought the wipers would distract drivers and make them crash.

Write the sentences correctly.

1. Everybody crys some times, but you don't has to be sad to cry.

   _____

2. Crying is actualy healthy, because tears clean your eyes and made you feel best.

   _____

Complete the sentence with the correct modal auxiliary verb.

3. You _____ cry if you are allergic to your pet or if you have a cold.

   must   might   should

Circle the regular noun and underline the abstract nouns.

4. You can also have tears of happiness, pride, or joy.

Read the words that have similar meanings.

fix	to make something work properly again
mend	to repair a tear or hole in a piece of clothing
restore	to clean and repair something old and dirty so it looks like it once did

Complete each sentence with the word that has the most precise meaning.

1. My brother likes to _____ old cars and make them look brand new.

2. Mom used her new tools to _____ the leaky faucet.

3. Dad said the huge hole in my pants is too big to _____.

Write a paragraph using all three words from the box.

4. _____

_____

_____

_____

_____

_____

Write the sentences correctly.

1. the loudliest land animal is the howler monkey, who's howls can be heard for miles.

_____

2. The monkeys use a loud voice so its group knows where they is.

_____

Write the adjectives in the correct order.

3. The call of the monkeys can be heard through the _____ forest.

                                                                         thick tropical   tropical thick

Complete the sentence with the correct preposition.

4. These monkeys like to stay _____ their small groups.

                  within   beneath   toward

Write the sentences correctly.

1. Although people cannot hear blew whales, they is the loudest water animal.

_____

2. The sounds these type of whale makes is louder than a jet engine.

_____

Complete the sentence with an antonym for *painless*.

3. If we could hear this whale, the sound would be _____ to our ears.

Complete the analogy.

4. whale : water animal :: monkey : _____

Write the sentences correctly.

1. After you read these sentence about yawning, you might yawn yourselves.

_____

2. Seeing someone yawn or even think about yawning, can make you yawn, too

_____

Use context clues to figure out the meaning of the bold word root. Then circle the meaning.

3. We may not be sure why people yawn, but it is an **act**ion that happens all the time.

    a. to see   b. to do   c. to pull

Underline the idiom in the sentence. Then explain what the idiom means.

4. The next time you yawn, look around, because seeing is believing.

_____

_____

Write the sentences correctly.

1. Long ago, native americans slept in tents as a way of life.

_____

2. Today, sleeping out doors under tents is called camping and much people love it.

_____

Circle the determiner that tells how often something happens.

3. Millions of Americans camp at parks every year.

Circle the meaning of the bold word.

4. Although it's a simple activity, people who take camping **trips** often take lots of gear.

    a. stumbles or falls   b. journeys

Read the definitions.

a. to cause a change in someone or something

b. the result of an action

c. proper; suitable

d. a basic law or belief

e. the job or duty of a person or thing

f. basic; the most important part of something

Write the letter of the definition next to each bold word.

1. function _____   consequence _____   appropriate _____

   affect _____   fundamental _____   principle _____

Write three sentences using three words from number 1.

2. _____

_____

3. _____

_____

4. _____

_____

Write the sentences correctly.

1. Robots are machines that purform jobs for peoples.

_____

2. People who have robots might use it to explore vacuum mow lawns or build things.

_____

Complete the sentence with the synonym for *copy*.

3. Robots can't think, but they can _____ the actions of a human being.

                        watch   imitate   study

Complete the spelling of the bold word.

4. Most robots work in **factor**_____, but some work underwater and in space.

              ys   ies

Write the sentences correctly.

1. One of the goodest books I've read is called a giraffe and a half.

_____

2. These book uses rhymes to tell about a boy and its pet giraffe.

_____

Add punctuation to the sentence.

3. The book starts with the words if you had a giraffe and he stretched another half ...

Complete the sentence with the words that are related to the bold word.

4. This book is very **creative** because of the _____.

                  fun rhymes and drawings   size of the words

Write the sentences correctly.

1. "Tomorrow, we creating a list of school rules," the Principal stated.

_____

2. "This rules will help students, teachers, and all of we to respect each other," she said.

_____

Complete the sentence with the word that means *the condition or state of being fair*.
Then circle the affix.

3. "A way to show respect is to treat everyone with _____," she said.

                                              fairness   fairly   fairer

Use context clues to figure out the meaning of the bold word. Then write the meaning on the line.

4. "If the rules aren't followed," she said, "the **consequence** will be staying after school."

_____

Write the sentences correctly.

1. The earlier pies in history are made mostly of meet.

_____

2. Today, people eat pie mainly for dessert but pie used to be eated all day long.

_____

Complete the sentence with the correct relative pronoun.

3. Maria Ann Smith is the person for _____ the Granny Smith apple is named.

                                     whom   who

Complete the sentence with the word that is most precise.

4. Most Americans _____ apple pie over any other kind of pie.

       prefer   like   enjoy

Read the words.

show	help	peculiar
odd	reveal	assist

Match pairs of synonyms. Write each pair on the lines next to each other.

1. _____ _____

   _____ _____

   _____ _____

Complete each sentence with a pair of synonyms from number 1.

2. After I _____ kids a magic trick, I _____

   how the trick is done.

3. I _____ Mom with the yard work and she _____

   me with my homework.

4. The zombie caterpillar is an _____ animal, but the zombie worm

   is even more _____.

Write the sentences correctly.

1. Hamberger hut have the bestest burgers in town and the fries are yummy, too.

_____

2. I wented there for lunch earlyer today and satted at my favorite seat.

_____

Write the word that best completes the sentence.

3. I _____ at the menu, but I already knew what I wanted to order.

glanced   peeked   stared

Rewrite the sentences to make one sentence.

4. I ordered a cheeseburger. I don't like ketchup, onions, or tomatoes.

_____

Write the sentences correctly.

1. Heat from the sun caused water on earth to turn from likwid into gas.

_____

2. The gas rise to the sky, and the water vaper became clouds.

_____

Complete the sentence with the correct word. Then circle the suffix that means _the act of_.

3. The act of water turning from liquid into gas is called _____.

evaporating   evaporated   evaporation

Circle the meaning of the bold word.

4. Water evaporates, clouds form, rain falls, and then the **cycle** continues.

a. a set of actions that happen over and over   b. a bicycle or motorcycle

Write the sentences correctly.

1. Zombie werms don't have teeth, mouth, or stomach.

_____

2. How do zombie worms eat bones? a person might ask.

_____

Use context clues to figure out the meaning of the bold word. Then write the meaning on the line.

3. The worm's skin makes large **quantities** of acid that breaks down bones.

_____

Circle the synonym of the bold word.

4. Scientists have found about twenty **types** of zombie worms, but there may be more.

    species   names   schools

Write the sentences correctly.

1. Meerkats are animals that has a sistem for help its group find food.

_____

2. One meerkat climes to the top of the high rock and bark if there is danger.

_____

Underline the words that have the same root. Then write the meaning of the root on the line.

3. Meerkats live in a communal society and rely on communication to survive.

_____

Circle the meaning of the bold word.

4. Meerkats can survive in desert heat because they've **adapted** to their environment.

    a. left an area because of heat   b. changed to suit a new purpose

Read the relative pronouns. Notice how they are used.

relative pronoun	how it is used
who	used with the subject pronouns **he, she**
whom	used with the object pronouns **him, her**
whose	used with the pronouns **his, her, their** to show possession

Read each question. Write a pronoun to complete the answer. Use the chart if you need help.

1. **Who** is having a party? _____ is having a party.

   With **whom** are you going to the party? I'm going with _____.

   Whose party are you going to? I am going to _____ party.

Write the relative pronoun that best completes each sentence.

2. To _____ did you send a party invitation?
       who   whom   whose

3. _____ is coming to your party?
   Who   Whom   Whose

4. I wonder _____ party you will go to.
       who   whom   whose

Write the sentences correctly.

1. If you want to learn to do karate, their are many schools who offer classes.

_____

2. Haveing a good karate teacher is importent to you're success.

_____

Complete the sentence with the best modal auxiliary verb.

3. You can look for a school on the Internet or you _____ visit a class in your area.

                                                    can   must   have to

Rewrite the sentences to make a complex sentence. Use the subordinating conjunction _if_.

4. Visit a class. You can meet the teacher and ask lots of questions.

_____

Write the sentences correctly.

1. The very first Earth Day was on april 22 1970, in san francisco california.

_____

2. At Earth Day, people think about ways to treet the planet best.

_____

Circle the meaning of the bold word.

3. One way to help is to **hold** a recycling day in your town or at your school.

    a. to have something in your hand   b. to arrange and take part in

Write the word that best completes the sentence.

4. If you are _____, you can come up with a way to save the planet.

    friendly   inventive   careful

Write the sentences correctly.

1. "The mall is giveing away free movie tikets in won hour," my friend said.

_____

2. "The malls far away but if we move fastly we can make it," I said.

_____

Underline the idiom. Then explain what the idiom means.

3. "Hold your horses," my friend said. "I can't go until I fix the pedals on my bike."

_____

Write the adjectives in the correct order.

4. "I think it's time for you to get rid of that _____ bike," I said.

old junky   junky old

Write the sentences correctly.

1. Arbor Day is a day where people show that you care about trees.

_____

2. People in most countrys spent the day hikeing, plant seeds, and read books.

_____

Use context clues to figure out the meaning of the bold word. Then write the meaning on the line.

3. People who want to help save trees can give money, or they can **contribute** their time.

_____

Complete the analogy.

4. nurture : care for :: conserve : _____

Read the similes and metaphors.

Hint: A simile uses the words *like* or *as* to compare two things.

A metaphor does not use the words *like* or *as*.

> a. The stars are diamonds in the sky.
>
> b. The water in the pool is as cold as ice.
>
> c. The snow is a white blanket.
>
> d. My sisters are like two peas in a pod.

Sort the expressions by similes and metaphors. Write the letters on the lines. Then write what each expression means.

1. similes

   _____ _____

   _____ _____

2. metaphors

   _____ _____

   _____ _____

Write one simile and one metaphor of your own.

3. _____

   _____

4. _____

   _____

Write the sentences correctly.

1. People use to make products with they hands but it took too much time.

_____

2. Bildings called factories was invented so that products could be made more fast than before.

_____

Complete the sentence with the best word.

3. In factories, machines are used to _____ products.

    handle   manufacture   complete

Complete the sentence with a word that means _someone who operates_.

4. A worker who operates a machine is called a machine _____.

Write the sentences correctly.

1. Poison ivy is a plant who's leaves has a oil that can make people itch.

_____

2. If you are exploreing in the woods and you see these plant, stay away

_____

Use context clues to figure out the meaning of the bold word. Then circle the meaning.

3. First you have to learn to **identify** poison ivy.

    a. to recognize   b. to stay away from

Write the adjectives in the correct order.

4. In spring, the poison ivy plant grows groups of _____ leaves that are red.

    three shiny   shiny three

Write the sentences correctly.

1. Today in hour science class, we done an expiriment with celery.

_____

2. We pored water onto a glass, added red dye over the water, and placed the celery between the glass.

_____

Use context clues to figure out the meaning of the bold word. Then write a synonym for the bold word.

3. When my teacher asked me what I **observed**, I said that the celery leaves turned red.

_____

Use context clues to figure out the meaning of the bold word. Circle the meaning.

4. She said that the celery turned red because it **absorbed** the colored water.

     a. did not like   b. soaked up or sucked up

Write the sentences correctly.

1. Spiders have ate legs so they are not insects.

_____

2. A spiders web is made from stickie silk threads that catches food.

_____

Use context clues to figure out the meaning of the bold word. Then write the meaning on the line.

3. If a web does not catch enough food, the spider **abandons** the web and makes a new web somewhere else.

_____

Write an antonym for the bold word.

4. Some people think that dusty old cobwebs are **beautiful**. _____

Read the phrase and its meanings.

> cut out   a. to form or shape by cutting
>
>   b. to stop doing something
>
>   c. to be well-suited for an activity

Which meaning of the phrase *cut out* is used in each sentence? Write the letter on the line.

1. For Valentine's Day, the students cut out paper hearts for decorations.   _____

2. Not everyone is cut out to be an Olympic athlete.   _____

3. My dad cut out soda from his diet because it has too much sugar.   _____

Write a paragraph using at least two different meanings of the phrase *cut out*.

4. _____

_____

_____

_____

_____

_____

Write the sentences correctly.

1. Dr. Jane Goodall is knowed for her studys of wild chimpanzees.

_____

2. In July, 1960, Jane Goodall wented to africa to lived with the chimps.

_____

Complete the sentence with the word that is most precise.

3. Jane knew the importance of protecting the apes' _____.

                                               surroundings   home   habitat

Complete the bold word with the prefix that means _to cause to be_.

4. Jane works to help apes and all animals that are _____**dangered**.

                                   en   non   mis

Write the sentences correctly.

1. In my school, we has a choyce of fun things to do.

_____

2. On Monday, we can play baloon games and on Wensday, theres a baking contest.

_____

Write the base word of the bold word.

3. On Fridays, we have a singing **competition**.   _____

Write the best word to complete the sentence.

4. If you are _____ and love to sing, you should enter the contest.

     quiet   strong   musical

Write the sentences correctly.

1. "I want to compleat these sewing project today," I telled my mom.

_____

2. "i'll make your lunch when you want a brake," she said.

_____

Underline the adage. Then explain what the adage means.

3. When Mom came to get me for dinner, I said, "Time flies when you're having fun!"

_____

Circle the two synonyms in the sentence.

4. "I'm certain you're having fun, but I'm also convinced that you're hungry," Mom said.

Write the sentences correctly.

1. I seen the outside of the white house before but I've never gotted to go inside.

_____

2. You can went inside the house for a tour but you must first ask permission.

_____

Complete the sentence with a word that means _to approve before_.

3. Before you visit the White House, a member of Congress must _____ your visit.

Write the best word to complete the sentence.

4. If you ask at least three weeks before you go, you will be _____ to go inside.   authorized   told   asked

Read the prepositional phrases.

> around the corner   under the bed   beside the tree
>
> over the fence   across the sky   on the roof

Write the prepositional phrase that best completes each sentence.

1. Let's run to the ice-cream truck _____.

2. We played ball and then we rested _____.

3. The big fluffy clouds are moving _____.

Write a paragraph using at least three of the prepositional phrases from above.

4. _____

_____

_____

_____

_____

_____

Write the sentences correctly.

1. "You need to makeup the test you mist while you was out sick," my teacher said.

_____

2. Sam and nancy rose their hands and sayed they would help me.

_____

Rewrite the sentences to make one sentence.

3. "Read chapter two in your book. Study with a partner," my teacher said.

_____

Complete the sentence with the relative pronouns _who_ and _whom_.

4. "_____ can lend me his or her book and with _____ can I study?" I asked

Sam and Nancy.

Write the sentences correctly.

1. My two best friends birthdays are on saturday and sundae.

_____

2. Im going to surprise them with a special desert called dirt cake.

_____

Write the correct word or words to complete the sentence.

3. This cake is fun to make and even _____ to eat.

                              funner   more fun

Rewrite the sentence to make a complex sentence.

4. You need to use chocolate cookies for dirt and pudding for mud besides using gummy worms.

_____

Write the sentences correctly.

1. Had you ever wanted a fresh peace of fruit in winter, but there wasn't none.

_____

2. If you has a greenhouse, you can grow plants fruit and flowers all year long.

_____

Use context clues to figure out the meaning of the bold word. Then write the meaning on the line.

3. A greenhouse is a **structure** with a glass or plastic roof that lets in sunlight.

_____

Draw a line between the prefix and the root word of the underlined word. Then write the meaning on the line.

4. Even if you are a beginner, a greenhouse will <u>enable</u> you to enjoy gardening.

_____

Write the sentences correctly.

1. A volcano is a mounten with a opening in the top of it.

_____

2. Volcanos have enuf power to change the way Earths surface looks.

_____

Underline the word that has a root that means _to break or burst_.

3. When an active volcano erupts, it sends gases and rock high into the air.

Complete the sentence with a superlative adjective.

4. While it's true that we have big volcanoes on Earth, the _____
   volcano is on Mars.   big

Read the relative adverbs. Notice what they tell about.

relative adverb	tells about
why	a reason
when	a time
where	a place

Write the relative adverb that best completes each sentence.

1. That is the store _____ I bought my shoes.

2. The reason _____ she is upset is that she lost her key.

3. I remember the time _____ we went fishing and caught a tire.

Write a paragraph using at least two of the relative adverbs from the box.

4. _____

_____

_____

_____

_____

_____

Daily Language Review • EMC 582 • © Evan-Moor Corp.

Write the sentences correctly.

   1. One of the most enjoying things to be done is fly a kite.

      _____

   2. Some times its not that easy to fly a kite so I will give you some tips.

      _____

Use context clues to figure out the meaning of the bold word. Then write the meaning on the line.

   3. Check the weather to make sure you have **sufficient** wind, or the kite will not fly.

      _____

Write the best word to complete the sentence.

   4. Find a _____ where there is a lot of room to run.

      field   forest   building

Write the sentences correctly.

   1. One of the famouser Parrots in the world was alex the African Grey parrot.

      _____

   2. Alexes owner spended many years train and study him.

      _____

Rewrite the sentences to make one sentence.

   3. Alex knew more than one hundred words. He was able to count. He could name colors.

      _____

Circle the synonym for the bold word.

   4. Alex and his owner **accomplished** many goals during Alex's life.

      imagined   believed   achieved

Write the sentences correctly.

1. Benjamin Franklin was an inventer that studyed electricity.

_____

2. There is a story that in June, 15 1752, mr. Franklin flied a kite on a stormy day.

_____

Complete the bold word with a suffix that means _referring to_.

3. He did an experiment to prove that lightning was **electric**_____.

                                       al   ful   er

Circle the meaning of the bold word.

4. He learned that the electrical **current** in lightning could start a fire, so he invented the lightning rod.

   a. something happening now   b. a flow of electricity

Write the sentences correctly.

1. Last month, I broke a leg, a ankel, and a elbow when I falled off my bycicle.

_____

2. The Doctor whom treated me said I couldn't go anywear for eight weeks.

_____

Write the best word to complete the sentence.

3. I felt so much pain, I just lay in bed and _____ in misery.

               whispered   moaned   laughed

Underline the idiom. Then explain what the idiom means.

4. When I couldn't sit up to play video games, I felt even more down in the dumps.

_____

Read the paragraph.
Use context clues to figure out the meaning of the underlined words.

> I went shopping for new shoes today. The shoe store
> had a big <u>variety</u> of shoes in all different colors and
> styles. I wanted to buy a <u>particular</u> pair of shoes that
> were red with blue stars. A friendly clerk who was
> <u>eager</u> to help me brought out ten boxes of shoes and
> even helped me try them on. Shopping for shoes
> made me so <u>weary</u>, I went home without shoes and
> took a nap.

Draw a line to match each word to its definition.

1. variety   worn out, tired

    particular   a number or collection of different things

    eager   specific

    weary   having or showing interest

Underline the part of the sentence that gave you the context clue.

2. The shoe store had a big <u>variety</u> of shoes in all different colors and styles.

3. I wanted to buy a <u>particular</u> pair of shoes that were red with blue stars.

4. Shopping for shoes made me so <u>weary</u>, I went home without shoes and took a nap.

Write the sentences correctly.

1. I think that some childrens should be politer.

   _____

2. Some childrens' manners aint good.

   _____

Complete the sentence with the best modal auxiliary verb.

3. When a child asks for a snack, she should ask, "_____ I have a snack?"

                                                Could   May   Should

Complete the sentence with an antonym for the bold word.

4. A **polite** child is nice to be around, but a _____ child is not.

Write the sentences correctly.

1. In 1776, the thirteen u.s. colonys decide they did not want to be part of england.

   _____

2. Five mans writed a letter that is called the declaration of independence.

   _____

Write the adjectives in the correct order.

3. The letter included _____ statements about the rights of people.

                   important three   three important

Circle the abstract noun.

4. After the letter was signed, the colonies had their own government and their freedom.

Write the sentences correctly.

1. "I can do a dubble flip off the diveing board," mark announces.

_____

2. "I thinked you was ascared of hi places," I said.

_____

Complete the sentence with the best word.

3. "I used to be afraid, but now I'm an expert diver," he _____.

    shouted   muttered   boasted

Underline the idiom. Then explain what the idiom means.

4. "Okay, then, show me a dive, because actions speak louder than words," I said.

_____

_____

Write the sentences correctly.

1. "A new skatebored shop are opening at the mall today," my friend said.

_____

2. "They are give away stickers hats and T-shurts," he said.

_____

Write the words that form the present progressive verb tense.

3. "Right now I _____, so I can't go," I replied.
    am studying   will be studying   was studying

Circle the prepositions. Underline the prepositional phrases.

4. "I can wait until you are done, or we can go tomorrow after school," he said.

Read the bold topics and the related words.

Earth Day	**animals**	**space**
conserve	adapt	astronaut
environment	habitat	gravity
recycle	species	planets

Match each definition to its related word from the box. Write the word on the line.

1. **definition:** to change old products into new ones so they can be reused

   word: _____

2. **definition:** the home of an animal

   word: _____

3. **definition:** a force that pulls objects toward each other

   word: _____

Write one sentence. Choose a word from one of the categories in the box.

4. _____

   _____

Write the sentences correctly.

1. For my school report, I choosed the topic of how Apes behave.

   _____

2. I wented to the san diego zoo so I could close watch them apes.

   _____

Use context clues to figure out the meaning of the bold word. Then write the meaning on the line.

3. When I got to the ape house, I saw the apes **exhibit** actions that seemed human.

   _____

Circle the meaning of the bold root.

4. I wrote five para**graph**s about what I saw and heard the apes do.

   a. to write   b. to hear   c. to see

Write the sentences correctly.

1. Your eyes gives you many information about a world.

   _____

2. Eyes sent information about movments colors and shapes to your brain.

   _____

Use context clues to figure out the meaning of the bold word. Then circle the meaning.

3. Our eyes are made up of many parts, including the lens and the **pupil**.

   a. the main opening of the eye   b. a student in school

Complete the analogy.

4. eyes : sight :: ears : _____

Write the sentences correctly.

1. People who drive cars must use good judgement, and follow a few safty rules.

_____

2. A driver should not drive too closely to the car in front of them.

_____

Complete the bold word with a word root that means *foot*.

3. Drivers must watch out for _____**estrians** who are crossing the street.

Use context clues to figure out the meaning of the bold prefix. Then circle the meaning.

4. If you are driving over the speed limit, you should **de**crease your speed.

   a. down   b. wrongly   c. over

Write the sentences correctly.

1. I found a baby bird who felled out of it's nest but it weren't hurt.

_____

2. It's Mother was nearby, and watch me close.

_____

Complete the sentence with the relative adverbs *where* and *when*. Use each word once.

3. _____ you find a bird, it's best to leave it _____

you found it.

Rewrite the sentence to make a compound sentence.

4. You might think you are helping. Taking a bird from the wild is not a good idea.

_____

Read each bold root and its meaning.

rupt	break, burst
terr	land
tract	pull, drag

Complete each bold word with a word root from above.

1. Dad uses a _____**or** to move dirt and snow off the road.

2. My sister always **inter**_____ Mom when she talks on the phone.

3. Baby porcupines stay with their mother for about six months before they find

   their own _____**itory**.

Write a paragraph using two of the words you made. Then underline the roots.

4. _____

   _____

   _____

   _____

   _____

   _____

Write the sentences correctly.

1. Wild animals cant go to a animal Doctor like a pet cat or dog.

_____

2. Studys show that wild animals who are hurt or sick can make theyselves better.

_____

Complete the sentence with a synonym for the bold word.

3. When wild animals need a _____ for their sickness, they find a **remedy** in nature.

Complete the sentence with the bold homophone that has the appropriate meaning.

4. Animals use leaves, roots, and seeds to _____ themselves.

   heel: the back part of the foot   **heal:** to make well again

Write the sentences correctly.

1. One thing that make firefighters brave is that they save peoples lifes.

_____

2. Regular people like me and you does brave things, to

_____

Circle the abstract noun.

3. If something you want to do is scary but you try to do it anyway, you are showing bravery.

Underline the simile. Then explain what the simile means.

4. When I got on an airplane for the first time, I was scared, but after the plane took off,

   I felt as brave as a lion.

_____

Write the sentences correctly.

1. "I need to hurry at Jims house before he leeves without me," I told my Dad.

   _____

2. "Do you remember what you say when you ask for a new puppy," Dad asked.

   _____

Complete the sentence with the best modal auxiliary verb.

3. "Yes. I promised I _____ feed and walk him every day," I said.

   might   would   could

Complete the sentence with the best word.

4. "I know you'll be _____ and walk Bo before you go," Dad said.

   brave   responsible   friendly

Write the sentences correctly.

1. "It's time to play the game called name your favorite TV cartoon," miss Gee told the class.

   _____

2. "The first two students to name his or her favorite cartoon would get a sticker," she said.

   _____

Complete the bold word with the ending that is spelled correctly.

3. "*Happ_____ Is a Warm Blanket, Charlie Brown!*" I called out.

   yness   iness

Add punctuation to the sentence.

4. Quick Miss Gee said Name the boy who didn't want to give up his blanket

Read the words with similar meanings.

dose	the measured amount of something to be taken at one time
portion	the amount of food served to a person at a time
slice	a piece of food cut from something larger

Complete each sentence with the best word.

1. Mom gave me one _____ of cold medicine and told me to rest.

2. I ate two chicken wings and one _____ of pepperoni pizza.

3. You may have one burger and one small _____ of french fries.

Write a paragraph using all three words from the box.

4. _____

_____

_____

_____

_____

_____

Write the sentences correctly.

  1. the empire state building opened on May 1 1931.

_____

  2. The Building is located at 350 Fifth Avenue New York New York

_____

Circle the word that is most closely related to the bold word.

  3. The building is one of the most **recognizable** buildings in the world.

    dangerous   beautiful   familiar

Rewrite the sentence so it is not a run-on sentence.

  4. The lights on the tower change color special occasions like Valentine's Day.

_____

Write the sentences correctly.

  1. Fables are short stories whos main characters is animals that talk.

_____

  2. A fable such as "the frogs and the well" teach readers a valueable lessen.

_____

Rewrite the sentences to fix the sentence fragment.

  3. When two frogs find a deep well. One frog wants to jump in, but the other frog says no.

_____

Underline the proverb. Then explain what the proverb means.

  4. This fable teaches that it is important to be wise and look before you leap.

_____

Write the sentences correctly.

1. Objects that is made from klay is called pottery.

_____

2. Much of the objects maded are useful but others are for decoration only.

_____

Complete the bold word with a word root that means *to shape*.

3. Clay starts as soil, but when it gets wet, you can **trans**_____ it into different shapes.

port   form   fer

Complete the sentence with the word that is most precise.

4. One way to shape clay is to _____ it as you would dough.

press   knead   rub

Write the sentences correctly.

1. Most roller coasters has no engine to push it along the track.

_____

2. A chain pulls the roller coaster to the top of the hill and then it flys down the track.

_____

Complete the sentence with an antonym for the bold word.

3. You feel **calm** on the way up, but on the way down you feel _____.

Write the best word to complete the sentence.

4. I always _____ with excitement when I ride a roller coaster.

shriek   bellow   roar

Read the word and its different meanings.

> **note** a. to notice; to observe
>
> b. a short letter
>
> c. a musical sound or symbol

Which meaning of *note* is used in the sentence? Write the letter on the line.

1. I wrote a thank-you note for the birthday present I received. _____

2. If you play a note on the piano, I'll sing you a song. _____

3. My teacher noted that I was late for class. _____

Write a paragraph using two of the meanings of the word *note*.

4. _____

_____

_____

_____

_____

_____

Write the sentences correctly.

1. The next time your hungry, think about haveing a termite sanwich.

   _____

2. You may knot know that many people around a world all ready eat insects.

   _____

Complete the sentence with the superlative form of the adverb *commonly*.

3. The _____ eaten insect is the beetle.

Use context clues to figure out the meaning of the bold word. Then circle the meaning.

4. Even though many insects are **edible**, most Americans do not want to eat them.

   a. something that is harmless   b. something that can be eaten

Write the sentences correctly.

1. Corals is ancient animals that live in under water communitys called reefs.

   _____

2. Coral reefs are finded where the ocean water is clear and the whether was warm.

   _____

Use context clues to figure out the meaning of the bold word. Then circle the meaning.

3. Tiny plants that live inside the corals need sunlight to **produce** food and survive.

   a. to make or manufacture   b. food that has been grown

Complete the sentence with an antonym for the bold word.

4. Corals must live in clear, **shallow** water because sunlight can't reach them in

   _____ water.

Write the sentences correctly.

1. Dr. Seuss real name was theodor seuss geisel and he was not really a Doctor.

_____

2. the cat in the hat And green eggs and ham is only two of his famous books.

_____

Use context clues to figure out the meaning of the bold word. Then circle the meaning.

3. Dr. Seuss drew **curious** creatures that had wild hair and wore tall, funny hats.

a. strange, unusual   b. wanting to learn or know more

Complete the bold word with the suffix that means _related to_.

4. His stories were like poems and were written in a **poet**_____ style.

ness   ful   ic

Write the sentences correctly.

1. If you was to build a park and a factorie in your sity, where would you put it?

_____

2. If your job title was city planner, youd plan how to made a city the nice place to live.

_____

Use context clues to figure out the meaning of the bold word. Then write the meaning on the line.

3. One job of a city planner is to **determine** where different kinds of buildings should go.

_____

Circle the word that has a Latin root. Then write the root and its meaning on the line.

4. A city planner often has a vision of how a city can be a better place to live.

_____

Read the homophones and their meanings.

> **cite**   to refer to a book
>
> **sight**   the ability to see
>
> **site**   the place or setting of something

Write the homophone that best completes each sentence.

1. After you write your report, be sure to _____ the books you used to gather facts.

2. The old baseball field is the _____ of the new skateboard park.

3. The sense of _____ is the sense that allows us to see.

Write a paragraph using all three homophones.

4. _____

_____

_____

_____

_____

_____

➤ **For many open-ended items, other answers are possible. Accept any response that produces correct language and follows the directions.**

Day 1

1. "I saw a giant balloon in the sky this morning," Ben said.
2. "It was shiny and shaped like an egg," he said.
3. "That was a blimp you saw, and it was part of a parade," I told Ben.
4. "The blimp is named *Spirit of America*," I said.

Day 2

1. A circus is a group of many performers, animals, and clowns.
2. If you go to a circus, you might see clowns who are acting silly.
3. You will see colorful costumes at a circus, and you will also hear loud music there.
4. workers who sell things

Day 3

1. Americans eat more ice cream than anyone else in the world.
2. Vanilla, chocolate, and strawberry are popular flavors, but the most popular is vanilla.
3. adjective; they give more details about ice cream
4. crunchy

Day 4

1. My mom doesn't eat meat, and that makes her a vegetarian.
2. Sometimes Mom eats rice and beans or spaghetti with tomato sauce.
3. Mom eats lots of veggies, but she doesn't get bored because they are so tasty.
4. that

Day 5

1. c
2. b
3. a
4. Answers will vary.

➤ **For many open-ended items, other answers are possible. Accept any response that produces correct language and follows the directions.**

Day 1

1. Many children ride on a bus every day.
2. It's important to stay in your seat when a bus is moving.
3. must
4. careful

Day 2

1. My grandma made me a party dress, and she made me a school dress.
2. The dress for my party has big purple polka dots.
3. un|able; not able
4. b

Day 3

1. Riding a bike is fun, but there are many rules you have to follow.
2. You must always wear a helmet, whether you ride slowly or quickly.
3. re|view; to view again
4. wear

Day 4

1. You should wear the right kind of shoes when you play soccer.
2. If your shoes don't fit well, you might get hurt on the soccer field.
3. could
4. when

Day 5

1. brave
2. tries
3. tell
4. Answers will vary.

➤ **For many open-ended items, other answers are possible. Accept any response that produces correct language and follows the directions.**

Day 1

1. Last year on my birthday, I told my mom that I wanted to get a pet snake.
2. Even though she knew how badly I wanted a snake, she still said no.
3. at a pet shop
4. scares

Day 2

1. I can't wait to visit my friend on Saturday, April 5.
2. My friend lives on a farm where there are lots of geese.
3. run
4. harmed; hurt

Day 3

1. Our class is doing a play called <u>All My Friends Have Four Legs</u>.
2. My teacher, Mrs. Brown, asked me to be one of the main characters.
3. "I am glad you asked me," I said to Mrs. Brown. "I would love to be in the play."
4. When

Day 4

1. At Gatorland in Orlando, Florida, you can learn how to train an alligator.
2. If you visit Dinosaur World in Cave City, Kentucky, you can dig for fossils.
3. can
4. discover

Day 5

1. scent
2. sent
3. cent
4. Answers will vary.

➤ **For many open-ended items, other answers are possible. Accept any response that produces correct language and follows the directions.**

Day 1

1. Lions are big cats that are best known for their loud roar.
2. Did you know that a lion can be heard from five miles away?
3. Sometimes people capture lions because they want to save them from harm.
4. living under human care

Day 2

1. I asked my dad if he would let me start a pet-sitting business.
2. My dad said I could start a business if I got good grades.
3. adverb; it describes how my mom told me
4. harder

Day 3

1. You will take good pictures if you know how to use a camera.
2. If you practice a lot, you'll soon be a good photographer.
3. modern digital camera
4. pre|view; to view ahead of time

Day 4

1. For a class project, I wrote a letter to a famous person.
2. I picked a person who is very important to the United States.
3. to whom
4. The first sentence of my letter said, "I am very proud to write to a U.S. president."

Day 5

1. around
2. across
3. beside
4. Answers will vary.

➤ **For many open-ended items, other answers are possible. Accept any response that produces correct language and follows the directions.**

Day 1

1. Everybody in my family likes to listen to music.
2. My parents' favorite kind of music is jazz.
3. My sister and I stream music, but Mom and Dad listen to CDs.
4. a

Day 2

1. Wheat is one of the most important crops in the world.
2. There are seven main kinds of potatoes that grow in the United States.
3. winter, but
4. leafy green vegetable

Day 3

1. Did you know that there is a difference between bugs and insects?
2. While bugs' mouths work like a straw, insects chew their food.
3. able
4. a

Day 4

1. A man on TV said that it's raining cats and dogs, so I ran outside to look.
2. My sister said, "It can't really rain cats and dogs, but once it rained frogs in England."
3. scratchy voice
4. animal

Day 5

1. pulling your leg
2. let the cat out of the bag
3. hit the sack
4. Answers will vary.

➤ **For many open-ended items, other answers are possible. Accept any response that produces correct language and follows the directions.**

Day 1

1. People who set a world record do something better than anyone else.
2. If a person sets a world record, his or her name could be in the book Guinness World Records.
3. youngest
4. try

Day 2

1. At school, my friends and I pick up trash we find lying on the ground.
2. Litter is a big problem because it makes the school look bad.
3. worse
4. I made a flier that said, "Litter is not cool. Please don't pollute our school."

Day 3

1. If you want to make a memory box, you need string, glue, markers, and a box.
2. You'll also need a few pieces of tissue paper to decorate the box.
3. to keep for future use
4. ly

Day 4

1. On September 9, 1850, California became a U.S. state.
2. Today, the cities in California that have the most people are Los Angeles and San Diego.
3. settled
4. b

Day 5

1. loc
2. port
3. mot
4. Answers will vary.

➤ For many open-ended items, other answers are possible. Accept any response that produces correct language and follows the directions.

Day 1

1. When the children ran through the house, they were shouting loudly.
2. The children's babysitter said, "Stop! You must slow down and play quietly."
3. who
4. over

Day 2

1. Appleton, Wisconsin, is the city where I used to live.
2. We moved because my dad got a new job.
3. where
4. a

Day 3

1. I saw a poster at school that said "Enter the School Writing Contest."
2. I wrote a story about an elephant that can draw and paint.
3. to try to win
4. Writ|er; a person who writes

Day 4

1. Before there were trains, men and women rode horses or walked.
2. People wanted to move faster, so they invented trains that move on tracks.
3. b
4. speedier

Day 5

1. c
2. a
3. b
4. Answers will vary.

➤ For many open-ended items, other answers are possible. Accept any response that produces correct language and follows the directions.

Day 1

1. One of the most popular pets in America is the tropical fish.
2. If you want pet fish, you have to buy an aquarium, food, and decorations.
3. adjective; they describe the nouns in the sentence
4. to put together the parts of

Day 2

1. There are many interesting facts about camels, but some things people believe are not true.
2. Camels do have curly eyelashes, but they do not have water in their humps.
3. unpleasant
4. could

Day 3

1. It's a good idea to save your money so you can buy something you really want.
2. If you are a kid who wants to save money, you should get a piggy bank.
3. Underline: After school; to the bank; near the mall
4. felt wonderful

Day 4

1. I like being in Girl Scouts because we do lots of fun activities.
2. The very first group of scouts got together on March 12, 1912.
3. Promise
4. Underline: "girls discover fun and friendship."

Day 5

1. b
2. c
3. a
4. Answers will vary.

➤ **For many open-ended items, other answers are possible. Accept any response that produces correct language and follows the directions.**

Day 1
1. On the first day of school, my friends and I walked to school together.
2. Because I wore a new pair of shoes, my feet hurt and it was hard to walk.
3. embarrassed
4. not able to help yourself

Day 2
1. There are many ways for people to travel if they want to go somewhere.
2. In London, England, people ride on tall red buses.
3. Some people ride horses, elephants, and camels to go places.
4. trans|port; to carry

Day 3
1. "Mom, can we go to the library and check out some books?" I asked.
2. Mom said, "Yes, but you have to get ready quickly, because it closes soon."
3. a person who works in a library
4. signature

Day 4
1. A cuckoo bird eats insects, and its favorite type of food is the hairy caterpillar.
2. The most common bird on Earth is the chicken.
3. flight|less; unable to fly
4. smart

Day 5
1. nervous
2. painful
3. cheerful
4. full of pain; having feelings of being worried or afraid; happy, full of cheer

➤ **For many open-ended items, other answers are possible. Accept any response that produces correct language and follows the directions.**

Day 1
1. If you need something to do this summer, think about helping the community.
2. You could pick up trash on the beach or mow lawns in your neighborhood.
3. October 22, 2016
4. help him

Day 2
1. Next time you eat your vegetables, think about what you are eating.
2. Plants have lots of different parts that we can eat.
3. The parts of plants that we can eat include roots, stems, leaves, and seeds.
4. when

Day 3
1. If you want to laugh, you should read a book called The Big Joke Book.
2. When I read the book, I was laughing so hard that I was nearly crying.
3. b
4. longer, louder

Day 4
1. My family doesn't have a cellphone like many people's families do.
2. Our phone has a long cord, and we can't go outside to talk.
3. dis|like; do not like
4. c

Day 5
1. get, show, similar, hide, give, job
2. get/acquire, get/acquire
3. show, demonstrate
4. give/contribute, give/contribute

➤ **For many open-ended items, other answers are possible. Accept any response that produces correct language and follows the directions.**

Day 1

1. Summer vacation is a time when my sisters and I do many fun things.
2. We go to space camp, or we learn to play a sport like tennis.
3. big bright
4. free to do what you want without any worries

Day 2

1. Walt Disney was born on December 5, 1901, in Hermosa, Illinois.
2. Maybe you have seen Mickey Mouse or Goofy on your vacation to Disneyland.
3. lovable
4. replay

Day 3

1. Twins are two children who are born together.
2. Some twins look exactly alike but are very different in other ways.
3. short
4. impossible

Day 4

1. The twin boys in my class invited me to their birthday party.
2. One of the boys is my best friend, so I couldn't wait to go.
3. might
4. hope|ful; full of hope

Day 5

1. ped
2. act
3. vis
4. Answers will vary. Roots should be circled.

➤ **For many open-ended items, other answers are possible. Accept any response that produces correct language and follows the directions.**

Day 1

1. Pluto was once known as the smallest planet in the solar system.
2. In August 2006, scientists said that Pluto is too small to be a planet.
3. scope
4. view

Day 2

1. The invention that is the most famous is the wheel.
2. The telephone, car, and electric light bulb were also important inventions.
3. inventive
4. the only one; nothing like it

Day 3

1. Deserts are dry places that don't receive much rain.
2. Desert animals get their water from food and store the water in their bodies.
3. to continue to live or exist
4. Even if it doesn't have water, the kangaroo rat can survive in the desert.

Day 4

1. You don't need a lot of equipment to go fishing.
2. You do need a fishing pole to catch the fish.
3. license
4. b

Day 5

1. lend
2. donate
3. give
4. Answers will vary.

➤ **For many open-ended items, other answers are possible. Accept any response that produces correct language and follows the directions.**

Day 1

1. A girl in my class named Anna told me about her pogo stick.
2. Anna said, "If you'd like to, you may jump on it, but don't hurt yourself."
3. balance
4. Underline: encouraged

Day 2

1. Many poems rhyme, but there are no rules for writing poems.
2. Once I read a book that's called This Poem Doesn't Rhyme.
3. Circle: when
4. imagine

Day 3

1. If you could choose where you live, would you live near a farm, city, or beach?
2. Some people think that the beach is the best place of all to live.
3. peaceful
4. noisiest

Day 4

1. Pizza is made mostly of bread, cheese, and sauce.
2. Many people bake pizza in their oven and eat it when it's hot.
3. can
4. Underline: it's not healthful to eat too much pizza. Circle: Although pizza is tasty,

Day 5

1. simile
2. metaphor
3. simile
4. Answers will vary.

➤ **For many open-ended items, other answers are possible. Accept any response that produces correct language and follows the directions.**

Day 1

1. Dogs are known as a human's best friend, but cats can be as friendly as dogs.
2. In my opinion, people don't understand cats.
3. like to be alone
4. completely different from each other

Day 2

1. Noah Webster was a teacher who made it easier for students to learn to spell.
2. In early America, people spelled words in many different ways.
3. one American
4. easy

Day 3

1. The food that astronauts eat today is much better than it used to be.
2. The first space food came in tubes and looked like baby food.
3. Today, space food is tasty. The food is also healthful.
4. they; It takes the place of the word *astronauts* so that it doesn't have to be repeated. It makes the sentence easier to read.

Day 4

1. Recycling trash is one way to keep planet Earth healthy.
2. Maybe you have heard the saying "Reduce, Reuse, Recycle."
3. to make less in amount
4. protect

Day 5

1. president, honesty
2. dream, spaceship
3. child, fear
4. Answers will vary.

➤ **For many open-ended items, other answers are possible. Accept any response that produces correct language and follows the directions.**

Day 1

1. Have you ever played a card game called "Go Fish"?
2. Yesterday, I tried it for the first time, and now it's a favorite game of mine.
3. are taking
4. The first player asks, "Do you have any kings?" The second player says, "Go fish!"

Day 2

1. Cave people were the first humans to create art.
2. They painted animals on the walls of caves, but no one really knows why.
3. prove
4. art|ists; people who make art

Day 3

1. Fireworks were invented more than two thousand years ago.
2. People think that Marco Polo brought fireworks with him from China.
3. make
4. easier

Day 4

1. If you have a dog that acts really bad, you can take him to a school for dogs.
2. Your dog will quickly learn how to act nice and obey you.
3. dis
4. to work together

Day 5

1. sturdy
2. ascend
3. foolish
4. strong, not easily broken; to go up; not wise

➤ **For many open-ended items, other answers are possible. Accept any response that produces correct language and follows the directions.**

Day 1

1. Did you hear that Opposite Day is on January 25, 2016?
2. At many schools, there is a lot of silliness on this day.
3. While some kids wear their clothes backward, other kids eat breakfast for lunch.
4. exciting, fun

Day 2

1. Female owls are larger and heavier than male owls.
2. Owls have sharp beaks and claws to help them catch and eat their food.
3. Large white
4. should

Day 3

1. The Pilgrims sailed across the Atlantic Ocean on a ship called the Mayflower.
2. The Pilgrims spent two months at sea before they spotted land.
3. put up with; survived
4. getting a tooth pulled

Day 4

1. On Mount Rushmore, four U.S. presidents' heads are carved in rock.
2. The closest city to this monument is Keystone, South Dakota.
3. b
4. liquid

Day 5

1. compare, deny, concealed, automatic, uncertain, infrequent
2. revealed, concealed
3. constant/infrequent, constant/infrequent
4. uncertain, convinced

➤ **For many open-ended items, other answers are possible. Accept any response that produces correct language and follows the directions.**

Day 1

1. If you want to know about your home state, there's a website you can go to.
2. On the page called Student State Facts, I found out my state's nickname and bird.
3. largest
4. Although Des Moines is the capital of Iowa, the first capital of Iowa was Iowa City.

Day 2

1. Have you read the book <u>Alice's Adventures in Wonderland</u>?
2. The tale begins when Alice sees a rabbit that is wearing a coat and looking at a watch.
3. "Oh my ears and whiskers, how late it's getting!" says the rabbit.
4. down a rabbit hole; circle: down

Day 3

1. I think salsa is one of the yummiest foods there is.
2. The best salsa is made with tomatoes, onions, peppers, and spices.
3. gulp
4. spicier

Day 4

1. My mom is a cook at a restaurant called Time to Dine.
2. Mom buys the freshest ingredients she can find, so the food is delicious.
3. prepares
4. to help

Day 5

1. tele
2. scope
3. graph
4. Answers will vary.

➤ **For many open-ended items, other answers are possible. Accept any response that produces correct language and follows the directions.**

Day 1

1. Birds have small brains compared to ours, but they are smarter than you think.
2. Birds know that the best time to catch worms is before the sun comes up.
3. success|ful; having the correct or desired result
4. If you are early, you will be successful.

Day 2

1. Did you know that Do Something Nice Day is on October 5?
2. The two easiest things to do are smile at someone and say hi.
3. take out the trash
4. a

Day 3

1. Some animals make sounds that would surprise you.
2. Wolves cry like a baby, geese honk like a horn, and cats purr like the motor of a car.
3. There are many other animals that make funny sounds.
4. hippo, hungry stomach

Day 4

1. We're finally inside the National Museum of American History in Washington, D.C.
2. I can't wait to see the very first flag, but my sister wants to see Oscar the Grouch first.
3. exclaim
4. un|believ|able; hard to believe; incredible

Day 5

1. b
2. c
3. a
4. Answers will vary.

➤ For many open-ended items, other answers are possible. Accept any response that produces correct language and follows the directions.

Day 1

1. Snakes are found nearly everywhere in the world except Antarctica.
2. Some snakes live in the sea, some live underground, and some climb trees.
3. Snakes' tongues are useful because they help snakes feel and smell.
4. Circle: always, constantly; synonyms

Day 2

1. Maybe you don't chew gum, but the ancient Greeks did.
2. Chewing gum comes from trees and is one of the oldest candies in the world.
3. small rubbery
4. unnatural, artificial

Day 3

1. Humpback whales are known for their singing.
2. Scientists don't really know why whales sing or what their songs mean.
3. noisiest
4. motion|less; not moving

Day 4

1. I like to play the board game called Monopoly.
2. My friend's favorite games to play are checkers and tic-tac-toe.
3. were playing
4. Underline: jumped, knocked, decided, play; they tell about the action that is happening

Day 5

1. idiom; proverb; adage
2. I'm all ears.
3. Practice makes perfect.
4. When it rains it pours.

➤ For many open-ended items, other answers are possible. Accept any response that produces correct language and follows the directions.

Day 1

1. Uncle James offered to take me to the baseball game.
2. I thanked my uncle but told him I had to do chores before I could go.
3. might
4. Underline: better late than never; Getting somewhere late is better than not going at all.

Day 2

1. Oranges are a juicy citrus fruit that have a lot of vitamin C.
2. Oranges grow on trees in warm, tropical places such as Spain.
3. Columbus brought the first orange seeds to the New World in 1493.
4. healthiest

Day 3

1. One of the main jobs of the nose is to help us smell.
2. The human nose can smell many different odors.
3. Before air goes into your lungs, your nose warms the air.
4. breathe

Day 4

1. Every country has a flag as its national symbol.
2. Flags have many different features, including colors, designs, and writing.
3. three
4. whose

Day 5

1. argued, grumbled, announced, declared, shouted
2. Answers will vary.
3. Answers will vary.
4. Answers will vary.

➤ **For many open-ended items, other answers are possible. Accept any response that produces correct language and follows the directions.**

Day 1

1. "My friends are coming over for dinner tonight," my little sister said.
2. "What are your friends' favorite foods to eat?" Mom asked.
3. My sister handed Mom a note that said, "We would like mud pie for dinner."
4. a

Day 2

1. On August 5, 2012, a space robot traveled to Mars for an important mission.
2. The rover named Curiosity had cameras so that we could see what Mars looks like.
3. ment
4. Circle: *Curiosity*; write: curiosity

Day 3

1. Your body does a lot of jobs to keep you healthy.
2. When you are cold, your muscles move, and that makes your body shiver.
3. ment
4. freezing cold

Day 4

1. Hurricanes are major storms that make waves, wind, and rain.
2. A storm isn't called a hurricane until the winds are moving really fast.
3. ly
4. where

Day 5

1. should/ought to
2. may/might/could
3. must
4. can/could

➤ **For many open-ended items, other answers are possible. Accept any response that produces correct language and follows the directions.**

Day 1

1. The wolf is a member of the animal family that includes dogs and foxes.
2. Two well-known types of wolves are the gray wolf and the red wolf.
3. rarest
4. to live in

Day 2

1. On March 2, 1903, the golden poppy became the official flower of California.
2. Some people believe that the poppy is one of the most beautiful flowers in the world.
3. into; circle: into San Francisco Bay
4. Underline: are a sea of orange; poppies, sea of orange

Day 3

1. Would you like to explore the Temple of Trash exhibit?
2. You should visit the Trash Museum at 211 Murphy Road in Hartford, Connecticut.
3. locate
4. view

Day 4

1. Our school's soccer team is called the Gray Foxes because that's our state animal.
2. The team wants its name changed to the Pink Panthers.
3. We wanted colorful uniforms, so we chose a team name with the word "pink" in it.
4. will be writing

Day 5

1. squealed
2. concerned
3. proud
4. Answers will vary.

➤ **For many open-ended items, other answers are possible. Accept any response that produces correct language and follows the directions.**

Day 1

1. My grandma and grandpa have a farm where there are daily jobs to do.
2. They make sure the animals have food, water, and a clean sleeping area.
3. to gather, to pick
4. b

Day 2

1. "I can do these puzzles faster than you can," I said to my friend.
2. "Let's race to see who finishes first," my friend replied.
3. dis
4. Underline: two heads are better than one; Two people can usually solve a problem better than one person.

Day 3

1. Men have invented many things, such as the car, the sewing machine, and peanut butter.
2. Women have invented many things, too, but we've only heard about a few of them.
3. c
4. Underline: distract; circle: tract

Day 4

1. Everybody cries sometimes, but you don't have to be sad to cry.
2. Crying is actually healthy, because tears clean your eyes and make you feel better.
3. might
4. Circle: tears; underline: happiness, pride, joy

Day 5

1. restore
2. fix
3. mend
4. Answers will vary.

➤ **For many open-ended items, other answers are possible. Accept any response that produces correct language and follows the directions.**

Day 1

1. The loudest land animal is the howler monkey, whose howls can be heard for miles.
2. The monkeys use a loud voice so their group knows where they are.
3. thick tropical
4. within

Day 2

1. Although people cannot hear blue whales, they are the loudest water animals.
2. The sounds this type of whale makes are louder than a jet engine.
3. painful
4. land animal

Day 3

1. After you read this sentence about yawning, you might yawn yourself.
2. Seeing someone yawn or even thinking about yawning can make you yawn, too.
3. b
4. Underline: seeing is believing. If you can see it with your own eyes, it must be true.

Day 4

1. Long ago, Native Americans slept in tents as a way of life.
2. Today, sleeping outdoors in tents is called camping, and many people love it.
3. every
4. b

Day 5

1. e, a, b, f, c, d
2. Answers will vary.
3. Answers will vary.
4. Answers will vary.

➤ **For many open-ended items, other answers are possible. Accept any response that produces correct language and follows the directions.**

Day 1
1. Robots are machines that perform jobs for people.
2. People who have robots might use them to explore, vacuum, mow lawns, or build things.
3. imitate
4. ies

Day 2
1. One of the best books I've read is called A Giraffe and a Half.
2. This book uses rhyme to tell about a boy and his pet giraffe.
3. The book starts with the words, "If you had a giraffe and he stretched another half…"
4. fun rhymes and drawings

Day 3
1. "Tomorrow, we will be creating a list of school rules," the principal stated.
2. "These rules will help students, teachers, and all of us to respect each other," she said.
3. fairness; circle: ness
4. the result of an action

Day 4
1. The earliest pies in history were made mostly of meat.
2. Today, people eat pie mainly for dessert, but pie used to be eaten all day long.
3. whom
4. prefer

Day 5
1. show, reveal; help, assist; odd, peculiar
2. show, reveal
3. assist, helps OR help, assists
4. odd, peculiar

➤ **For many open-ended items, other answers are possible. Accept any response that produces correct language and follows the directions.**

Day 1
1. Hamburger Hut has the best burgers in town, and the fries are yummy, too.
2. I went there for lunch earlier today and sat in my favorite seat.
3. glanced
4. I ordered a cheeseburger without ketchup, onions, or tomatoes.

Day 2
1. Heat from the sun causes water on Earth to turn from liquid into gas.
2. The gas rises into the sky, and the water vapor becomes clouds.
3. evaporation; circle: ion
4. a

Day 3
1. Zombie worms don't have teeth, a mouth, or a stomach.
2. "How do zombie worms eat bones?" a person might ask.
3. amounts
4. species

Day 4
1. Meerkats are animals that have a system for helping their group find food.
2. One meerkat climbs to the top of the highest rock and barks if there is danger.
3. Underline: communal, communication; together, with
4. b

Day 5
1. He/She
   him/her
   his/her/their
2. whom
3. Who
4. whose

➤ **For many open-ended items, other answers are possible. Accept any response that produces correct language and follows the directions.**

Day 1

1. If you want to learn to do karate, there are many schools that offer classes.
2. Having a good karate teacher is important to your success.
3. can
4. If you visit a class, you can meet the teacher and ask lots of questions.

Day 2

1. The very first Earth Day was on April 22, 1970, in San Francisco, California.
2. On Earth Day, people think about ways to treat the planet better.
3. b
4. inventive

Day 3

1. "The mall is giving away free movie tickets in one hour," my friend said.
2. "The mall's far away, but if we move fast, we can make it," I said.
3. Underline: Hold your horses; Hold on, wait
4. junky old

Day 4

1. Arbor Day is a day when people show that they care about trees.
2. People in most countries spend the day hiking, planting seeds, and reading books.
3. to give
4. save

Day 5

1. b: The water in the pool is very cold.
   d: My sisters are a lot alike.
2. a: The stars are bright like diamonds.
   c: The snow covers the land like a white blanket.
3. Answers will vary.
4. Answers will vary.

➤ **For many open-ended items, other answers are possible. Accept any response that produces correct language and follows the directions.**

Day 1

1. People used to make products with their hands, but it took too much time.
2. Buildings called factories were invented so that products could be made faster than before.
3. manufacture
4. operator

Day 2

1. Poison ivy is a plant whose leaves have an oil that can make people itch.
2. If you are exploring in the woods and you see this plant, stay away.
3. a
4. three shiny

Day 3

1. Today in our science class, we did an experiment with celery.
2. We poured water into a glass, added red dye to the water, and placed the celery in the glass.
3. saw, noticed
4. b

Day 4

1. Spiders have eight legs, so they are not insects.
2. A spider's web is made from sticky silk threads that catch food.
3. leaves
4. ugly

Day 5

1. a
2. c
3. b
4. Answers will vary.

➤ **For many open-ended items, other answers are possible. Accept any response that produces correct language and follows the directions.**

Day 1

1. Dr. Jane Goodall is known for her studies of wild chimpanzees.
2. In July 1960, Jane Goodall went to Africa to live with the chimps.
3. habitat
4. en

Day 2

1. At my school, we have a choice of fun things to do.
2. On Monday, we can play balloon games, and on Wednesday, there's a baking contest.
3. compete
4. musical

Day 3

1. "I want to complete this sewing project today," I told my mom.
2. "I'll make your lunch when you want a break," she said.
3. Underline: Time flies when you're having fun! Time goes quickly when you're doing something you enjoy.
4. Circle: certain, convinced

Day 4

1. I've seen the outside of the White House before, but I've never gotten to go inside.
2. You can go inside the house for a tour, but you must first ask permission.
3. preapprove
4. authorized

Day 5

1. around the corner
2. beside the tree
3. across the sky
4. Answers will vary.

➤ **For many open-ended items, other answers are possible. Accept any response that produces correct language and follows the directions.**

Day 1

1. "You need to make up the test you missed while you were out sick," my teacher said.
2. Sam and Nancy raised their hands and said they would help me.
3. "Read chapter two in your book, and then study with a partner," my teacher said.
4. Who, whom

Day 2

1. My two best friends' birthdays are on Saturday and Sunday.
2. I'm going to surprise them with a special dessert called dirt cake.
3. more fun
4. Besides using gummy worms, you need to use chocolate cookies for dirt and pudding for mud.

Day 3

1. Have you ever wanted a fresh piece of fruit in winter, but there wasn't any?
2. If you have a greenhouse, you can grow plants, fruit, and flowers all year long.
3. building
4. en|able; to let someone do something

Day 4

1. A volcano is a mountain with an opening in the top of it.
2. Volcanoes have enough power to change the way Earth's surface looks.
3. Underline: erupts
4. biggest

Day 5

1. where
2. why
3. when
4. Answers will vary.

➤ For many open-ended items, other answers are possible. Accept any response that produces correct language and follows the directions.

Day 1

1. One of the most enjoyable things to do is fly a kite.
2. Sometimes it's not that easy to fly a kite, so I will give you some tips.
3. enough
4. field

Day 2

1. One of the most famous parrots in the world was Alex the African Grey parrot.
2. Alex's owner spent many years training and studying him.
3. Alex knew more than one hundred words, was able to count, and could name colors.
4. achieved

Day 3

1. Benjamin Franklin was an inventor who studied electricity.
2. There is a story that on June 15, 1752, Mr. Franklin flew a kite on a stormy day.
3. al
4. b

Day 4

1. Last month, I broke a leg, an ankle, and an elbow when I fell off my bicycle.
2. The doctor who treated me said I couldn't go anywhere for eight weeks.
3. moaned
4. Underline: down in the dumps; feeling sad

Day 5

1. variety: a number or collection of different things
   particular: specific
   eager: having or showing interest
   weary: worn out, tired
2. Underline: all different colors and styles
3. Underline: red with blue stars
4. Underline: took a nap

➤ For many open-ended items, other answers are possible. Accept any response that produces correct language and follows the directions.

Day 1

1. I think that some children should be more polite.
2. Some children's manners are not good.
3. May
4. rude, impolite

Day 2

1. In 1776, the thirteen U.S. colonies decided they did not want to be part of England.
2. Five men wrote a letter that is called the Declaration of Independence.
3. three important
4. Circle: freedom

Day 3

1. "I can do a double flip off the diving board," Mark announced.
2. "I thought you were scared of high places," I said.
3. boasted
4. Underline: actions speak louder than words; What you do is more important than what you say.

Day 4

1. "A new skateboard shop is opening at the mall today," my friend said.
2. "They are giving away stickers, hats, and T-shirts," he said.
3. am studying
4. Circle: until, after; underline: until you are done, after school

Day 5

1. recycle
2. habitat
3. gravity
4. Answers will vary.

➤ **For many open-ended items, other answers are possible. Accept any response that produces correct language and follows the directions.**

Day 1

1. For my school report, I chose the topic of how apes behave.
2. I went to the San Diego Zoo so I could closely watch the apes.
3. do, perform
4. a

Day 2

1. Your eyes give you much/a lot of information about the world.
2. Eyes send information about movements, colors, and shapes to your brain.
3. a
4. hearing

Day 3

1. People who drive cars must use good judgment and follow a few safety rules.
2. A driver should not drive too close to the car in front of him or her.
3. ped
4. a

Day 4

1. I found a baby bird that fell out of its nest, but it wasn't hurt.
2. Its mother was nearby and watching me closely.
3. When, where
4. You might think you are helping, but taking a bird from the wild is not a good idea.

Day 5

1. tract
2. rupts
3. terr
4. Answers will vary.

➤ **For many open-ended items, other answers are possible. Accept any response that produces correct language and follows the directions.**

Day 1

1. Wild animals can't go to an animal doctor like a pet cat or dog.
2. Studies show that wild animals that are hurt or sick can make themselves better.
3. cure
4. heal

Day 2

1. One thing that makes firefighters brave is that they save people's lives.
2. Regular people like you and me do brave things, too.
3. Circle: bravery
4. Underline: as brave as a lion; Even though she was scared, she felt brave after she did it.

Day 3

1. "I need to hurry to Jim's house before he leaves without me," I told my dad.
2. "Do you remember what you said when you asked for a new puppy?" Dad asked.
3. would
4. responsible

Day 4

1. "It's time to play the game called Name Your Favorite TV Cartoon," Miss Gee told the class.
2. "The first two students to name their favorite cartoon will get a sticker," she said.
3. iness
4. "Quick!" Miss Gee said. "Name the boy who didn't want to give up his blanket."

Day 5

1. dose
2. slice
3. portion
4. Answers will vary.

➤ **For many open-ended items, other answers are possible. Accept any response that produces correct language and follows the directions.**

Day 1
1. The Empire State Building opened on May 1, 1931.
2. The building is located at 350 Fifth Avenue, New York, New York.
3. Circle: familiar
4. The lights on the tower change color for special occasions like Valentine's Day.

Day 2
1. Fables are short stories whose main characters are animals that talk.
2. A fable such as "The Frogs and the Well" teaches readers a valuable lesson.
3. When two frogs find a deep well, one frog wants to jump in, but the other frog says no.
4. Underline: look before you leap. Before you act, you should think about the dangers/consequences.

Day 3
1. Objects that are made from clay are called pottery.
2. Many of the objects made are useful, but others are for decoration only.
3. form
4. knead

Day 4
1. Most roller coasters have no engine to push them along the track.
2. A chain pulls the roller coaster to the top of the hill, and then it flies down the track.
3. excited, afraid
4. shriek

Day 5
1. b
2. c
3. a
4. Answers will vary.

➤ **For many open-ended items, other answers are possible. Accept any response that produces correct language and follows the directions.**

Day 1
1. The next time you're hungry, think about having a termite sandwich.
2. You may not know that many people around the world already eat insects.
3. most commonly
4. b

Day 2
1. Corals are ancient animals that live in underwater communities called reefs.
2. Coral reefs are found where the ocean water is clear and the weather is warm.
3. a
4. deep

Day 3
1. Dr. Seuss's real name was Theodor Seuss Geisel, and he was not really a doctor.
2. The Cat in the Hat and Green Eggs and Ham are only two of his famous books.
3. a
4. ic

Day 4
1. If you were to build a park and a factory in your city, where would you put them?
2. If your job title was City Planner, you'd plan how to make the city the nicest place to live.
3. figure out
4. Circle: vision; vis, to see

Day 5
1. cite
2. site
3. sight
4. Answers will vary.